TINY
Miracles

TINY
Miracles

A Mother's Journey
of Finding Faith through
Childhood Cancer

Jennifer F. Hendricks-Fogg

Foreword by **SARA ORTON,**
Development Director at Children's Healthcare of Atlanta

For my supportive husband, Kevin,
for being my rock on this journey.

And for Logan, you are a real-life superhero
and will always be our tiny miracle.

CONTENTS

FOREWORD

"YOUR CHILD HAS CANCER." These are words no family should ever have to hear. And yet, according to the Children's Oncology Group, more than sixteen thousand families each year will hear those words. Each diagnosis is different, each family is different, but many things are the same. The dedication, perseverance, and strength it takes to navigate a cancer diagnosis is always tremendous.

I have come to know many families who have been impacted by pediatric cancer in my ten-plus years of working for the Aflac Cancer and Blood Disorders Center of Children's Healthcare of Atlanta (CHOA). Each time

I am introduced to a mom, a dad, a sister, or a brother my heart breaks for them because I know the hardships of the road they are already traveling (or the road they are about to embark on).

I once read a quote that said, "If your path is difficult, it is because your purpose is bigger than you thought." I think about this often when I am reminded of Kevin, Jennifer, and Logan. Their journey has been more than difficult, but as you will learn by reading their story, they are destined for bigger things. They are larger than cancer.

I was first introduced to Jennifer through our work with Aflac. Then, in 2017, I was visiting New York for business, and I asked Jennifer if I could stop by and say hello. That first meeting took place in the waiting room at Albany Medical Center. Since that day I have known how special Jennifer is—and not just because of her story but because of her determination. If you know Jennifer, you know exactly what I am talking about. Shortly after that first meeting with Jennifer, I then met Logan. At the time he was a small, fearless warrior who defied the odds, showed us he was a rock star, and made all of us proud. (And he continues to do so to this day.)

March 8, 2017 is a day that will forever define Logan. This was his diagnosis day; the day when the world shifted for his entire family—and let's be honest, an entire community. That day was followed by years of treatments, surgeries, therapy, hospital stays, setbacks, and still many milestones. If you have walked a path like the one Logan and his family have traveled then you know how lonely, challenging, and monumentally difficult it can be.

What I continue to be proud of and inspired by is Jennifer's fierce love and protection for her son. Of course, every mother loves her child, but when you're put in a situation like Jennifer was, I cannot help but think your love means something more. Your dreams and wishes for your child's future are put on the back burner as you work through a new reality to simply keep your child alive.

A cancer diagnosis is a long, difficult, and often painful road, and it takes a village to navigate. Each of you reading this book are part of Logan's village. Only through advocacy and awareness will we shed light on the need for more support for kids like Logan.

I hope you are as inspired by reading Logan's story as I have been in the years of knowing this special family. Not only are they fighting for Logan but they are also fighting to help other families through the Logan Strong Foundation. When you see the determination in Jennifer's eyes as she speaks about Logan, you know she will not stop and will not settle—and for that, I am thankful. I am honored to call Kevin and Jennifer my friends, and each day Logan serves as a reminder that our work will never be done until we have better treatment options and a cure for every child diagnosed with this horrific disease.

—**SARA ORTON**, Development Director
at Children's Healthcare of Atlanta

INTRODUCTION

WHEN YOU DREAM of having a child, you imagine all the things they will do—play on the swings, run in the park, play sports, share your favorite foods, read bedtime stories, and so much more. The words "childhood cancer" are not even in your vocabulary. You never think it is going to happen to your family.

My son, Logan, was diagnosed with a brain tumor at just three and a half months old. To say that we were devastated and blindsided would be accurate, and yet a total understatement. All of the dreams we once had for our baby boy were shattered, leaving behind a storm of questions: *WHAT?!*

How do babies get cancer? How did this happen? What are we going to do? So many emotions, thoughts, and doubts entered our minds.

Cancer. With that one word, our lives have been changed forever. I firmly believe that everything happens for a reason, and as much as this journey has sucked (for the most part), I'm certain it was meant to happen, and I know that Logan chose my husband and me to be his parents for a reason. I half-joke and say that Logan chose me to be his mother because I have a big mouth and I get shit done! (Okay, that's no joke!) But seriously, I know that I was meant to be Logan's mom, and over the years I've learned to bring my resilience and my mother's intuition into battle with me every time I've had to fight for my son.

While we may have been through hell and back—and we're still struggling with the aftermath of cancer—Logan continues to strive, survive, and overcome any worst-case scenario that comes his way. My husband and I have been reshaped by this experience too. We're constantly learning and growing personally, professionally, and in our relationships with one another.

We will never know what it's like to have a "normal" child. And before you tell me there is no such thing as "normal," let me say this: you are right, but what I see as "normal" is a child without cancer; a child who can walk, talk, and eat on their own. I will never know what it's like to see my child walk across the living room for the first time, or experience what it's like to feed my child spinach baby food, or watch him play in the backyard by himself. These "normal" milestones were stolen from my family. But Logan has had so many of his own incredible moments. Over and over again, he has proven that miracles *do* happen, and that my little boy is stronger than I could have ever imagined.

I have a story to tell—a story of fear and faith, of a mother's fierce love, and her child's determination to destroy the odds and fight for his life. Logan is a miracle child, and while he still may have a way to go with his development, I have no doubt that he will overcome and keep proving them all wrong! He has a story to tell, and I'm here to share that story with you, through my eyes. (While this book is about my personal reflections through my son's cancer journey, I acknowledge that some of the content may be triggering to those who are or have been in similar—or even not-so-similar—circumstances. Please know that I am in no way comparing or judging anyone else's attitudes toward a situation. This is my story—and my feelings—alone.)

To be honest, I struggled with trying to start writing this book because I was afraid of reliving the emotions of those first few years. It all felt so overwhelming, and I didn't even know where to start; I just knew I had so much to say. *Do I start with how I got married late in life and tried to conceive? Do I start with the day we found out Logan had fluid on his brain? Do I start with the day he was diagnosed with cancer?* I didn't know what to do, and for a while I was stuck in the confusion. But our story is such a powerful one, and I knew I just had to get it out. When I thought about all that Logan has gone through, I was reminded that we are each stronger than we think. And just like Logan has overcome, his mama can too!

Finding the time to write this book was another story! My schedule is extremely limited—I am a special-needs mom, I'm home with Logan every day after school, I work part-time, and I run the Logan Strong™ Foundation (supporting other local families with a childhood cancer diagnosis). Not to mention bringing Logan to his additional therapies every week, going to doctors' appointments and IEP meetings, meeting with his case manager, filling out paperwork, etc. But let's be honest: nobody has the time; we have to *make it*. One of my favorite sayings is, "People make the time for things that are important to them, or they make excuses." I was done making excuses for not writing this book. As hard as I knew it would be, I was excited to be on this journey. I knew it would be healing for me, and it is my hope that our story will resonate and provide hope and faith for others to know that miracles *do* exist!

While trying to write this introduction, I've been interrupted at least a dozen times. Between stopping to feed Logan (he's 100 percent tube-fed), taking him to the bathroom (we are currently potty training), being hit or attacked by him (I'll explain this more throughout the book), bringing him downstairs to play in his ball pit, and finally laying him down for a nap, I've snatched every opportunity to work and write in those precious moments in between. This is just part of my reality—it's how I get everything done, and this book is no exception.

Today is July 4, 2021, and we will be heading to a friend's camp for a pontoon boat ride followed by a barbecue and fireworks, which Logan loves! I can't think of a better day or way to kick off the writing of this book. I am so excited to share our journey with you.

Logan is such an amazing kid. He is super smart and gorgeous—and that's not being biased (okay, maybe a little).

With every challenge that he overcomes, he continues to teach us lessons of hope, love, and strength. And in hearing our story, I hope you can share in that wisdom too. I hope you will learn to see the miracles in your own life, to hold on to hope, and believe that anything is possible. I hope Logan's story will empower you to defy your own limits and find the strength to get through whatever comes your way.

I also hope this book will bring to light the brutal reality of childhood cancer, and the lack of funding and research for a cure. Every year, nearly sixteen thousand children in the US are diagnosed with cancer. That's *thousands* of children who will have to face the overwhelming pain and struggle of fighting cancer, just like Logan has. My goal is to raise awareness with this book and with our work through the Logan Strong Foundation. If you find you want to take steps to help, I've provided more information in the "How to Help" section on page 245.

Be advised that this book will contain foul language and gut-wrenching truths. I am a very open and honest person; I tell it like it is, and I don't hold back. This is a story of faith, miracles, grief, pain, loss...you name it, it's in here! So have your tissues ready... (I've got mine right next to me.) Here we go!

CHAPTER

1

IT'S JULY 7, 2021. We've just finished Logan's weekly feeding therapy session and there was not a dry eye in the house! Logan fed himself a spoonful of water *and* swallowed it, *three times*! Yes, that is cause for excitement in this house! Logan has been getting some type of feeding or speech therapy since he was first diagnosed in 2017. After his second brain surgery—which removed 50 percent of his tumor and left frontal lobe—he stopped taking food by mouth. The left frontal lobe controls language development, motor skills, personality, and impulse control. And if you met Logan, you would know that all of those areas have been affected—except his personality! Regardless of his traumatic brain injury (TBI), Logan really is a good kid!

But back to today's feeding therapy session... We have been seeing McKenzee Greene, Logan's speech-language pathologist, since January 2020. We had been going one or two times a week for a few months, took a short break when COVID-19 hit, and then went back strong for a few months. McKenzee, being the professional she is, sat me down one day in August 2020 and told me that she had some news to share. I knew in my gut that she was going to tell me she was leaving the facility. She had alluded to it a few times prior, and with things ever-evolving and changing with COVID, she had found a new job with better hours, more benefits, and higher pay. I was genuinely happy for her but I was very upset that we were losing her. She had been so good with Logan, and with his TBI and developmental delays, consistency is hugely important for him. Before I even had a chance to ask her to stay, she said, "I told my new job that the only way I would take the position is if I could keep one private client." I knew she meant Logan, and I just started bawling my eyes out. I was so relieved and extremely grateful.

Logan has that effect on people. He is so smart and so cute. Even when he's upset or pissed off during therapy, he could have tears rolling down his cheeks, but he will still push through and complete the task. He had been working so hard in his sessions and had finally just gotten comfortable with holding a spoon. I was so afraid that after the eight months we had spent with McKenzee, if we had to switch therapists, he would regress. So, even through COVID (minus some quarantines here and there), McKenzee has been coming to our house—pro bono, I might add—since August 2020. She is working on getting licensed with CDPHP (a local health insurance company) and Medicaid, so once she's fully accredited, she will definitely be getting paid. We even offered to self-pay and she wouldn't take it. Again, that's the effect Logan has on people. So, after a year and a half of consistently working with McKenzee, Logan willingly took a sip from a spoon *on his own*! Can you say "BFD" (big fucking deal)?

That's actually one of the exciting things about this journey. The little things he does, whether they're normal for his age or they're just what kids do, are amplified! Knowing and saying all his shapes and colors was *huge*. They told us he would probably never walk, and now the kid runs circles around us. So, yeah, the day he started walking was another BFD! Logan has this special aura about him; he just pushes through, and you can see it in his eyes that he's really trying and wants to figure it out, whatever he is focused on. Because of his drive and determination, there is no such thing as the word "disability" in our vocabulary. We like to describe Logan as being "developmentally delayed," not "disabled." Being disabled means you are unable to do something, but being developmentally delayed means that you can do it, just on your own time. And boy, let me tell you, this kid is definitely on his own schedule. Patience is a real virtue around here!

While this may be the exciting side of things, there are always two sides to every situation, and there are days when I feel defeated, alone, and devastated. Fighting and beating cancer was nothing compared to the TBI and developmental delays we live with now because of where the tumor was. Don't get me wrong, Logan will overcome all these delays and will adapt with his TBI, but it is hard as hell! Having your toddler attack you or start banging his head because he lacks impulse control is frustrating. And I'm sure these things happen because he's frustrated too. He can't tell us what's wrong; he knows a ton of words but not enough to be able to communicate appropriately all the time. He's 100 percent tube-fed, so meals are often a struggle, and don't even get me started on the potty training!

Our daily routine is always an exercise in patience. I've got more scratches and bruises on my hands and arms than I can count. I've been headbutted—and I've bit my tongue a few times—and I even once had a black eye from my son. I know he doesn't mean it and he doesn't do it on purpose, but there are some days when it can push me to my limits. There are many times when I've lost it and just screamed in frustration. I love my son. I feel blessed and grateful to be able to be there for him through every obstacle. But this doesn't make it easy. It's hard, it's exhausting, and most days I'm fucking burned-out! *I am not OK. I am so alone. I have no one to talk to, no one to help with Logan. No one understands how I feel or what I go through.* These thoughts go through my head daily, and the weight of them can feel crippling at times. I am exhausted—physically, emotionally, and mentally. Yes, my husband is amazing, and he takes on so much for our family, but I'm the one who handles everything. (Yes, I'm a mom, and I like to be in control.) I schedule all the doctors' appointments, therapies, evaluations, and babysitters. It's all on me. Luckily, I have a flexible schedule where I am able to do all these things, but I'm exhausted. And yet, even when I'm exhausted, I look at Logan, my miracle child, and I am so grateful that I get to be his mom and watch him conquer every limitation that is placed on him.

Yes, my son is amazing. He is a miracle, and he has overcome every worst-case scenario. But that doesn't mean it's easy...it's not! There are so many things that I wish I could change for Logan. I hate that my child was born with cancer. I hate that he now has a brain injury from where the tumor was. I hate that he cannot feed himself and has difficulty communicating. I just want my son to be normal. I just want him to eat and play and talk and run like every other kid. Every four hours I have to stop what I am doing to feed him via his gastronomy tube (G-tube), and most times it's a straight-up fight to get him to sit still. He bites me, hits me, and pulls my clothes or my hair the whole time. I can't let him just go outside and play with other kids in fear that he will hit, bite, or headbutt them, or pull their hair. He's super smart, and he definitely understands more than we know, but the part of his brain that is injured regulates his impulse control which is where these issues lie. I can't send him to a regular day care because of this, and I can't find help to come into the home because I don't trust many people, the hiring pool is limited, and it takes a special person to be able to handle him. It may be crazy to fathom, but in some ways living in the hospital while my child was fighting cancer was easier than the life we live now. At the hospital, we had tons of people who were there to help us: doctors, nurses, child life specialists, family, and friends. At home now, it's just me and my husband. (And most days it's mostly me because my career allows for more flexibility than my husband's.)

I'm not sharing all of this with you because I want you to feel sorry for me, my husband, or Logan. I share this because I want you to take from this our messages of hope and faith. We don't plan for tragedy to come into our lives, whether it's an illness, the loss of a loved one, or a crisis of our own making. We can only do our best and put one foot in front of the other to push forward each and every day. I know I will get through this as I always do, but I will *never* get over what happened to Logan—and I will *never* lose hope that my child will continue to beat the odds. Our lives have been forever shaped by the journey you're about to read, and our story is one we could have never expected when my husband and I dreamed of having a child.

CHAPTER 2

MY ENTIRE LIFE, all I ever wanted to do was become a mother. As fate would have it, I didn't meet my husband until later in life, and we dated for several years before we got married. And by that point, I was afraid that my time would never come.

I first met my husband, Kevin, on Friday, January 14, 2011, when I was thirty-five years old. (Although, in all honesty, that's not completely true. I used to date one of his friends when I was eighteen, so that night wasn't *really* the first time we'd met.) By this time in my life, I had been through quite a few horrible relationships. I could write a whole other book on my choices in the wrong men (boys, really). I have been left in two different states—I moved out of state with one guy, and within a week, he was gone—I've had ten thousand dollars stolen from me, one guy stole my vehicle, and I've had the shit kicked out of me. With every guy I had dated, I thought he was "the one." (They never were.) I think I got this from my parents' relationship—they met in February of my mother's senior year of high school, got married that August, had me the following year, and were married for thirty-three years (until they divorced; I'll get there in a minute). I was always worried about everyone else, and I had always put my boyfriends' needs first. I never really focused on myself, which is strange because I'm an only child!

When I met Kevin, I was living at home with my father. He and my mother had recently split, and I had been living with not-so-great roommates, so I decided to move home. It was a win-win for my father and me. But what thirty-five-year-old single woman wants to hang at home every night? So I became a regular at O'Toole's, which was the local hangout—and ironically enough, it was my first job when I was eighteen when I worked there as a hostess—it's basically our local Cheers!

I remember exactly how it happened. I was at the bar

talking with my friend, Chris, who worked at FedEx. The FedEx terminal was down the road from O'Toole's so a lot of the guys would hang out there after work, and I knew a handful of them. The next thing I knew, Kevin walked up to me, wearing his FedEx uniform, and asked, "Are you Jen Hendricks?" My first reaction in my head was, *Yeah, why?* But I was polite and said yes. He then introduced himself and I said, "Oh, hi!" I knew his name from when I had dated his friend years ago, but I wouldn't have recognized him if I had tripped over him.

I had been just getting ready to leave, but I decided to buy Kevin a drink and catch up a bit. We had been chatting for a while and watching hockey on the TV when the owner of the bar came up to us and said he had two tickets to the New Jersey Devils hockey game in New Jersey that following Sunday. He asked if we wanted them. I had just gotten into watching hockey that year, and Kevin had been a hockey fan his whole life and even played a bit, so he and I looked at each other and said sure. I thought he was cute, I knew he was close to my age, and we had already discussed that neither of us had ever been married or had children. At thirty-five, it was hard to find someone who didn't have children or ex-spouses. Plus, we were both living at home at the time for different reasons.

Normally, if I liked a guy I would be very forward, and I'd let him know it right away. I am independent, outgoing, and very type A. But with Kevin, I decided to play my cards right. I immediately knew I wanted to take it easy, chill out a bit, and just see where it would go. It also helped that I knew I was going to see him that following weekend. Anyway, it worked. I didn't hear from him that weekend, but he called me that following Monday after work. We chatted for a while and made plans to grab a drink later that week so we could make arrangements for the weekend. He was going to a motorcycle show in New York City on Saturday with his best friend, Dan, and he invited me along so we could spend the night there and go to the hockey game the next day. We had just met and we were already going away for the weekend together...this could either make it or break it!

It was nice to see Kevin in his realm. He raced motorcycles and played hockey, so he was immediately bringing me into his world. He was not like any other guy I had dated, and honestly, he wasn't my type, but I really liked him. He was laid-back and easygoing; nothing bothered him. He is who he is, and he has always been content with that.

We dated for a while, and by the end of our first year together, he had practically moved in with my father and me. In March of 2012, he came home from work and said he had to get up early for a meeting the next day to learn about Aflac.

I said, "Oh, is it with Michelle?"

He said, "Yes, I think so."

I said, "Great, tell her I said hello." At the time, Michelle Nolan was a new district sales coordinator with Aflac. I had met Michelle a few years prior at a Chamber of Commerce networking event. She had targeted me from across the room and we clicked right away. Almost instantly, she tried to recruit me to come work with her. I had ultimately declined the offer because I couldn't afford to work for commission only, but Michelle and I had kept in touch, attending networking events together, grabbing lunch, and referring business to each other.

A couple of days after Kevin met with Michelle, we both met her for dinner and he signed up for his Aflac policies. Before the night was over, Michelle talked to me again about working for Aflac as an independent benefits consultant. I had been working in a job that I absolutely hated, so I thought, *Why not?* I was bartending part-time and teaching dance part-time while living at home so my expenses were low, which meant I could now afford to work on commission. I also liked the flexibility of the job, which would allow me to still teach dance two or three afternoons a week. I decided to then work toward getting my insurance license part-time at night while teaching dance two afternoons a week, bartending on Friday and Saturday nights, and helping a friend during the days with her local newspaper. Which, let me tell you, was fucking hard! But I made it work.

Within the first two years of my career with Aflac, I was a top sales associate and was able to quit bartending and my other part-time day job to focus on my career and teaching dance. Kevin and I also got our first apartment together, and after dating for three years, not only was my internal clock ticking but so was my patience for getting married. I wasn't even sure at that time if Kevin wanted to have kids, but I needed to get that ring first!

We had talked about getting married, and it was definitely our plan, but I was just waiting for the proposal. One day I noticed a bag from the jewelry store sitting on his dresser in the spare bedroom which was also my home office. *Very subtle—not!* The bag stayed there for about a week, and I kept waiting for him to ask me to dinner, plan a date, or do something, but nothing came of it. Then on Saturday morning, March 15, 2014, I came home from teaching dance, and as I was making myself lunch, I noticed Kevin was acting odd; he was very nervous and fidgety.

When I asked what was going on, he said, "Will you sit still? I'm trying to give you your ring!" (Yep, that's the romantic man I married!)

I actually yelled at him because we were going to his best friend's wedding that night, and I wasn't going to show up to the wedding with a new ring on my finger. Although, even without the ring, it was all I talked about that night at the wedding! After his friend's wedding, I figured he would do something romantic and give me the ring on the way home or even when we got home... *Nope, nothing.*

The next morning, I had to get up early for a meeting, and now I was the one who was fidgeting and acting nervous.

I finally yelled, "Can I have my ring please?!"

He complied and tried handing it to me.

I was like, "Wait, that's not how you do it!" I was over the whole romantic proposal thing because that's just not his style, but I still wanted some sort of gesture.

He said, "I don't know how to do this."

So, me being the type A person I am, I said, "Get on your

knee!" (And it didn't come out as nicely as you may have read that!)

He did, and he asked me, and of course, I said yes!

We got married a little over a year later, on June 20, 2015. Our wedding was so much fun! Our table numbers were actually trivia questions about some of our favorite things. Kevin loves trivia, so when our guests got their table cards, there was a question on the back of each card and the answer was the name of their table. Some of the tables were named after "Law & Order SVU," Bruce Willis, the New York Yankees, and the New York Rangers. The food was buffet-style, with different stations from our favorite restaurants. They were even able to duplicate some of our favorite foods from O'Toole's, where we had met. There was also a pasta station and a gelato station from our favorite Italian restaurant and bakery. My bridesmaids and I even did a flash mob! Our wedding was very memorable. We hit the trifecta, as I like to say. The wedding officiant was a friend of mine, whom I had known for years, and she called my husband by the wrong name—she called him Keith instead of Kevin. It's been a running joke for years now! Then my husband dropped my ring just as he was about to put it on my finger, and he dropped me during our first dance. He went to dip me and lost his balance, and me being the dancer I am, I went with it and made it very dramatic.

By the time we were married, I was thirty-nine years old, and I knew I was ready to talk about starting a family. As much as Kevin wasn't sure if he wanted kids or wanted to be a dad, I knew he wanted to make me happy. And at the end of the day, I knew in my heart that he would make an amazing father. We are so much alike but also very different, and each of our strengths would make us a great parenting team. He is the calm in the eye of my hurricane. So, after we got married, I went to the doctor to inquire about getting pregnant at my age. He said it was definitely possible, but if we weren't successful within six months, we would need to see a fertility specialist. Normally they wait one year before recommending fertility services, but time wasn't on our side.

After trying for six months to get pregnant with no success, we saw a specialist. We did all the testing, and there was nothing wrong with either of us. All of our bloodwork came back normal as well. The doctors decided to put me on a fertility plan. It was a trigger shot one day, intercourse within a couple of days, and then a pregnancy test two weeks later. It worked! On our first time around, we got pregnant. We were both so ecstatic!

My husband wasn't the type of guy to get married, none-theless have a baby. But he did it; *we* did it. I knew how much he loved me, and we wanted to start a family together. This was something that I had wanted my entire life, and yet it was something he hadn't known he wanted or needed until he met me.

There was no question that we both wanted to have a boy. I knew, as an only child—and a girl—that I had been a handful, and there was no way we could handle another me! Plus, having a boy meant continuing the family name, hockey, motorcycles, baseball, and of course, if he wanted to take dance classes, I was all for that too!

I still remember the day when we found out we were having a boy. The doctor had done all the genetic testing, and every-thing looked great. We then asked how soon before we could find out the sex, and the doctor said that they already knew and asked if we wanted to know. Without hesitation, Kevin and I looked at each other and said yes. When the doctor said it was a boy, we were even more elated. I had called my girlfriend, Ashley, on the way home (we were both pregnant at that time), and when she asked me what we were having, I replied with, "I hope you get your girl." She wanted a girl, and I wanted a boy. I think that comment gave it away!

We didn't tell anyone, and instead decided to save the news for our gender reveal party for which we had a cake made with blue frosting hidden in the center. It was so hard to keep our secret because we were both so excited to have a boy. I couldn't wait to dress him like a little man; I couldn't wait to be a #boymom, to watch my son take his first steps, play hockey, or ride a motorcycle (although that thought gave me great anxiety). I couldn't wait to just cuddle and snuggle all day long, to hear him laugh for the first time, and to hear him say, "Mommy"! I was so excited for all the firsts we were about to experience as a family.

I had always wanted twin boys and a girl (I know, totally random). I had wanted at least two kids because, as an only child, I know that when my parents go, I will be the only one left, and I didn't want my child to ever feel that way. I knew that this conversation would be tough to have with my husband because he was OK with having one kid. He is the middle of three boys, and he saw it from the opposite perspective of having hand-me-downs and being financially frugal. But having one boy at forty years old was a blessing in itself. And at that point I didn't care; I was just taking it one day at a time. We were pregnant—with a boy—and life was about to become more amazing than we ever could have imagined.

Boy, were we wrong...

CHAPTER
3

THROUGHOUT MY PREGNANCY I had several ultrasounds—more than most, due to my age, or as they call it medically, a "geriatric pregnancy." Guess it pays to be #40and-knockedup...you get extra photos of your unborn child!

Veteran's Day 2016 was on Friday, November 11. Kevin had the day off from work, but with my job, I worked a lot regardless of whether it was a holiday. By this point, I was just about eight months pregnant, and we were scheduled for yet another ultrasound.

We got to the ultrasound late. In fact, we were so late that they told us if we had been just one more minute late they would have canceled our appointment. Little did we know it at the time, but this would be the start to the universe/God/higher spirit (or whatever you want to call it) having our back throughout this entire journey.

We were brought into the room, got set up, and the technician did her thing, just as she had done every other time. After performing the ultrasound, she walked out to review the results with the doctor. Kevin and I had no inkling that there was anything wrong. The radiologist walked back in with the technician and informed us that there was fluid on our son's brain. I don't recall the radiologist's name, but I do recall being told that they had just transferred to the practice a week prior and had specialized in this exact thing. So, this would be the second time in one day that the universe had our backs.

Without fully understanding what we might be facing, we were concerned and extremely upset. Luckily, we had another appointment about an hour later with our family physician, Dr. Cozens, who was a young new physician from England. I had been seeing the same primary physician, Dr. Roche, at that office since I was twenty-two years old. I still joke with my doctor that he is the longest relationship I've ever had. So, when I got pregnant, I trusted him with choosing our ob-gyn/family physician. Several times during our regular appointments with Dr. Cozens, Dr. Roche had popped in on the visit. This day was no exception. Dr. Roche was one of the senior partners in the practice, so not only was he brought in for comfortability on my behalf, but also from a seniority standpoint.

As I was sitting on the table in the exam room, Kevin was sitting in the chair in front of me. He was very calm (or at least he appeared to be, from my perspective). He is not typically an emotional person, and he always does his best to stay strong for me. At this point, I was completely inconsolable over the news we had just gotten during the ultrasound. Dr. Roche and Dr. Cozens were talking when another doctor walked in: Dr. Mack. She was another senior partner of the practice whom I had never met before. She came over to me, and without saying a word, she put her hand on my shoulder. I immediately felt this unwavering sense of calm come over me. I had never met this woman before; she didn't know me or my history, and I obviously didn't know her. Honestly, I had never even seen her before, but there was this aura about her. She was quiet and calm, and I instantly trusted her. The kindness that she showed me that day with just that one touch had put me at ease. I didn't know a stranger's touch could have such an effect. To this day, whenever I see Dr. Mack, she always has the most genuine smile and asks about Logan and our journey.

After spending the better part of the day at the doctor's office, our medical team decided that further testing was necessary and that someone would call us on Monday to schedule an MRI. I was OK with the further testing, but waiting until Monday for a call was very unnerving.

Being told that we needed further testing on our unborn child was, at that time, the worst news we had ever heard. I felt a little at ease knowing that our doctors were comfortable with sending us home, but I was also highly concerned that they wanted to do more testing. *More testing for what? What could it be? Were they not telling us something? Were they waiting because it would just fix itself? What would have happened if we hadn't had the ultrasound?* So many questions were running through my head. But I had to stay positive. We hadn't come this far to not be able to handle anything that would be thrown our way. I could tell that Kevin was just as devastated as I was, but he was being strong for me and wasn't letting his emotions show or get the best of him.

That weekend, we tried to stay as busy as possible to keep ourselves distracted and not let our minds wander. I had a work celebration dinner that evening which we were supposed to go to, but I did not have the mental capacity to be "on" that night, not to mention that my eyes were swollen from crying all day. That Friday night, Kevin ended up going to the Union College hockey game and then out with friends, and I stayed home and had a couple of girlfriends over. I kept myself busy with work stuff that Saturday as it was my busiest time of year and there were always folders to be stuffed or organizing to do to get ready for the next week. We both went to another Union College game that Saturday night. And luckily, on Sunday, we had matinee tickets to see *Dirty Dancing* at Proctors Theatre in Schenectady, and then we went to a friend's house for dinner afterward.

Finally, we received a call on Monday, November 14, and my MRI was scheduled for the following week. I was not in any position mentally or emotionally to wait another week to find out what was going on with our son, so I reached out to a girlfriend who used to work for Albany Medical Center. She, in turn, reached out to one of her old coworkers to see what they could do to help. Sure enough, she was able to get us scheduled for an MRI that Thursday, November 17.

I was an emotional wreck that whole week. I was trying not to stress because I knew it wasn't good for the baby. But how was I supposed to not stress while knowing there was something potentially very wrong? I threw myself into my work that week and just tried to stay as busy as possible.

When Thursday rolled around, the hospital was over-booked so there was a tractor trailer parked outside that housed two MRI machines. That would be where I would have my MRI. I had had a few MRIs in my life before that day, and I recalled how uncomfortable and claustrophobic they can be. But now there I was, eight months pregnant, knowing how uncomfortable it would be, and to top it off, it would all be done in a cramped trailer. I was not very comfortable with the situation, but I knew it was necessary. As it turned out, that was the most uncomfortable MRI I had ever had. It was awful!

The doctors had told us that we would be hearing something from them as soon as they received the results from the radiologist. By six that evening, we hadn't heard anything, so I was feeling better about the situation. I figured that we would have heard something by five o'clock, end of business hours, if anything was not right. Well, I was wrong.

I received a phone call around seven from Dr. Mack. She said that they wanted to do more testing and asked if we were able to go to Albany Med in the morning to do so. I said of course! I did follow up with questions. (You know me, type A planner.) "Should I pack a bag for the baby? Should I pack a bag for myself?" She said it couldn't hurt. I knew right then and there that we were having our baby the next day. I hung up the phone and filled Kevin in on the conversation and said we would be having our baby tomorrow. He insisted they just wanted to do more testing, but I knew in my gut that I was having my son the next day.

We started making calls. Kevin called his parents who had recently moved to North Carolina. I called my mom and then my best friend, Colby (who is also Logan's godmother), and asked her to come over and help me pack. I hadn't done any packing yet; that had been on my to-do list for that next weekend. I also called my good friend, Bridget, whose husband is a trooper—and not in the sense that he handles things well; he's literally a state trooper. We needed to have the car seat installed and checked, and who better to do that than a trooper? I also had to call my regional coordinator for work. The fourth quarter is always the busiest time of year for my business, and my goal had been to work until one week before my due date. All in all, there was a lot to cover and juggle in less than twelve hours before we checked into the hospital at eight o'clock the next morning. To say I was nervous and scared would be an understatement.

I barely even slept that night. The next morning, we got to the hospital on time and we checked into the Labor and Delivery department. They brought us into a nice room where we got settled rather quickly. It was a private room with a cozy couch that was set in front of the window and visible straight ahead as soon as you walked into the room. There was also a small sink and cabinets to the right of the door, and the bed was in the middle of the room with a TV hanging on the wall. I immediately got comfortable in the bed, and I called my mother and my father while Kevin called his parents, just to let everyone know we had arrived and were waiting for further testing.

After a while, they brought me into a different room where they could do another ultrasound. My anxiety was through the roof, but I knew we were in the right place. Before I had even gotten pregnant, I knew that I wanted to give birth at Albany Med. I had been born there, and based on my age, I knew that if there was anything wrong with me or my child, I would already be in the best place because the Bernard and Millie Duker Children's Hospital is the only children's hospital in northeastern New York and western New England.

After I had returned from the ultrasound and was settled back into my room, the radiologist came in and gave us some devastating news. He told us that the fluid on Logan's brain was blood, and they thought he had something called (neonatal alloimmune thrombocytopenia (NAIT). As he described it, my platelets and my husband's platelets didn't fit together—and the prognosis wasn't good.

The radiologist told us our son would not survive.

I looked him dead in the face and said, "Fuck you. I didn't wait until I was forty years old to have my first child just for you to tell me he's not going to survive." That was *not* an option.

To this day, I don't remember that doctor's name, and I think maybe he's lucky I don't. He had a horrible bedside manner and was very crass.

"Take him out and fix him," I demanded.

A little while later, another doctor came in. He was in the fellowship program in the NICU department at the time—and a handsome man, I might add! He insisted we call him "Michael," not "Doctor," and because of that, I can't remember his last name to save my life. (Michael, if you are reading this, please know the tremendous impact you have had on our journey!) Michael was wonderful to speak to; he was very consoling, heartfelt, and honest. He said, "Look, we don't know what it is. It could be a million other things, but we won't know until we take him out and better examine him and run the proper tests."

This made me feel better. Even though he was a younger doctor, he was, in my opinion, more experienced with babies and their treatment, compared with a radiologist who just reads scans. His bedside manner alone was miles above the radiologists, and that was a selling point for me (sorry, I'm in sales, it's how I reference things). He was so easy to talk to, and he helped me come around to the fact that there were no true certainties at that point and they would have to take Logan out to do further testing. So rather than causing us to freak out any more than we already had, Michael was nurturing and sincere.

After talking some more, Michael and our medical team decided that the next best step was to have an emergency C-section. I was only thirty-five weeks and five days along, so I wasn't full-term, and there was still a risk that Logan's lungs wouldn't be strong enough. I was given a dose of steroids to help with his lungs, and Michael said it was up to us if we wanted to deliver that day or take another dose of steroids the next morning and deliver then. We asked him what the difference was, and he said it might help with a little more lung strength, but there have been other babies delivered at twenty weeks whose lungs were strong enough. We decided to have the emergency C-section that day.

We called everyone: my mother (who was already on her way), my father, Kevin's parents, and Colby. My mother and Colby were at the hospital within the hour. Colby later told me that when I had called her, she had been at the gym and had nearly fallen off the treadmill when I told her. Kevin's parents were in North Carolina and were getting on the road that afternoon to head up. My father was also on his way.

Prepping for an emergency C-section was overwhelming, to say the least. I was alone for most of the prep, and although I was very scared, the nursing staff and doctors were so comforting and understanding. Not knowing what was to come once Logan was born was terrifying. I was numbed from the chest down, and the doctors kept asking me if I felt a pinprick here or there, but I couldn't feel a thing. A drape was placed in front of me so that I couldn't see what was going on. It was kind of creepy as there was a mirror placed so that I could peek around the drape just a bit, although they eventually moved the mirror as the surgery got started.

Finally, Kevin was brought in, along with several other

doctors. Albany Med is a teaching hospital, so there were more people in the room than there would typically have been. Despite all the crowding and bustling, all I could think about was how I just wanted to hear my baby cry when he came out. I could overhear the head doctor instructing the students on what to do. When it came time to take Logan out of my stomach, the doctor said she would do it. They made my C-section incision a bit longer than they normally would because they were concerned with Logan's head.

At 2:29 p.m. Logan Daniel Fogg was born. (Daniel had been my grandfather's first name, and he died on August 22, 2002, on my twenty-sixth birthday. I always felt there was a reason why he had passed away on my birthday; a reason I am still unsure of. However, I knew that if I had a son, I wanted him to have my grandfather's name. And Logan Daniel it would be!)

When they took him out, he let out a big scream, and I felt like I could finally relax a bit. The next several hours were very trying! When they took Logan out of my belly they let me see him for a quick second. I got to snuggle him with my cheek for a few moments, and then he was gone. It was like a drive-by; here's your kid, and now we're taking him away again.

They brought him into a room that was about twenty feet away. Kevin was able to go into the room with them, and I just kept watching through the window in the door, trying to figure out what was going on and just continuing to pray that there would be smiles and affirmative head nods. I was so nervous. *What was going on? What was happening with my kid?* Not knowing was so scary!

After a little while, they took Logan to the NICU and brought me up to a room. Kevin stayed with Logan and the medical team. That was more important to me than him being with me; I had my mother and Colby there for me. But Logan needed his daddy! (To this day, that just makes me cry! Kevin is such a great dad, and he has been since day one, especially considering this was the guy who wasn't even sure if he wanted kids! We are truly blessed to have him!) Every mother wants to be the first to hold and bond with her baby, but that wasn't to be the case for us. This time it was daddy, and I was honestly OK with that. Kevin was spending time with Logan in the NICU while the doctors were still running tests. He was able to hold him, and he video chatted with me so I could see him.

I tried so hard to get up so I could go see Logan in the NICU, but I was so nauseous and lightheaded from all of the drugs and medicine I had been given for the C-section, I couldn't even get out of bed. I tried to force myself a few times, but it just wasn't happening. At one point, I walked very slowly to the bathroom, and I knew I was going to get sick. Colby was in the room with me at the time, and I yelled to her that she may want to leave. When she asked why, I told her I was about to get sick. She has emetophobia (the fear of vomiting), so she really appreciated the heads-up!

About eight hours later, I was finally able to be wheeled down to the NICU to see Logan. He was so tiny and so perfect. All I wanted to do was cuddle my baby and take him home to start our lives as a family of three. But Logan ended up spending five days in the NICU. The doctors continued to run tests to try to figure out what the brain bleed was. *What had caused it? Would it go away on its own? What type of treatment would he need?* All of these thoughts went through our heads, and Logan's doctors were wondering the same things. Logan was assigned a first-class medical team to help figure this out, including a pediatric oncologist/hematologist, Dr. Lauren Weintraub; a pediatric neurosurgeon, Dr. Matthew Adamo; a developmental pediatrician, Dr. Judith Lucas; and a pediatric neurologist, Dr. Charles Nichter.

Logan was also born with a hemangioma on his back, which showed up as a bright red birthmark on his lower back. It looked like a rubbery bump about one inch by three inches and was made up of extra blood vessels in the skin. Dr. Weintraub wasn't concerned and said Logan would grow out of it (which he eventually did). That eased our minds. Dr. Weintraub and Dr. Adamo worked together a lot, and they agreed that the brain bleed was just a birth defect, and he would grow out of that as well, but they still wanted to continue monitoring him. They also conferred with Dr. Lucas and Dr. Nichter and agreed to also start him on a physical therapy (PT) plan to get ahead of any physical developmental delays. We were comfortable with their expertise and their decisions, and we were so ecstatic to take our baby home!

We spent our first Thanksgiving and Christmas at home. It was wonderful! And on the day before New Year's Eve, we received amazing news at Logan's first follow-up MRI. The brain bleed was dissipating as the doctors had expected! Finally, we could breathe a little easier knowing our baby was on the mend. They wanted us to continue with PT, and it was agreed that they would continue to monitor Logan. We scheduled another follow-up MRI for March 8 of the following year and just continued to enjoy our newborn baby!

At the time, we had three pets: two dogs (Torre, a fourteen-year-old rat terrier, and Roxy, a nine-year-old puggle) and a cat (KC, short for kitty cat, because my husband and I couldn't agree on a name). Torre and KC could have cared less about having a new baby in the house, but Roxy became Logan's protector and never left his side. Any time we had company over and someone new was holding Logan, she was always within three feet of him. When Logan slept on the couch in his Boppy pillow, Roxy would be on the back of the couch sleeping as well, again, always within three feet of Logan. For a nine-year-old dog, Roxy was still very hyper and playful, but to see how she calmed down and took a motherly role with Logan was heartwarming—until she got really sick and we had to put her down in January 2017. The best way to explain all of this is with the letter I wrote to her...

Dear Roxy,

You were my best friend for almost ten years. You were by my side through many failed relationships, career changes, and homes. You were not only a good judge of character but were a character yourself. Always happy, hyper, and playful. You acted like a puppy your entire life, and although you annoyed the crap out of me at times, that didn't matter to you; you always loved me and wanted to cuddle and eat. Oh boy,

*did you eat! You acted like you were starving...all the time!
Where did you put it?!*

*When I met your dad, Kevin, you fell in love with him just as
quickly as I did, eventually becoming "Daddy's little girl." He
fell just as in love with you too. You were always by his side,
and it was clear how much you would rather be near him than
me. I was OK with that because we both had found the love of
our lives. He was (is) the best thing that ever happened to us!*

*You knew that all I ever wanted was to find the right guy, get
married, and start a family alongside finding a career that
I loved. You stuck by me as I found myself and these things
that I had always wanted. Thank you! I couldn't have done
it without you!*

*When your father and I finally got married and became preg-
nant with your brother, my life was exactly where I wanted it
to be; not to mention, my career was on the right track. Then
your brother was born a month early, via an emergency C-
section because they found a hemorrhage in his brain. I knew
God didn't get me this far just to take him away. Sure enough,
he is fine, and the hemorrhage is dissipating on its own.*

*Since the day when we brought Logan home, you were always
within three feet of him, especially if someone else was holding
him besides your father or me. It was apparent that you were
his protector. More so now than I ever could have imagined.*

Then one day, you started acting funny, had trouble walking, and were shaking constantly. We thought for sure it was a back injury because of the way you were always jumping on and off the couch, over things, etc. Little did we know, until after several vet appointments, that you had a malignant tumor that had corroded your bones, which was causing the shaking and your inability to walk. You had it for quite some time and were in a lot of pain. You never showed any signs. You knew that Daddy and I were focused on and worried about your brother, and you put us first. For that, I love you more than you could ever know (as tears flow down my face as I write this).

When we found out it was cancer, we had a talk that night. I told you to let me know when you were ready to go. I told you that you were my best friend and that I didn't want to see you in pain. Little did I know that the next morning you would tell me you were ready to go. You couldn't even stand up. I called the vet and they said it was worse than they had thought; it was inoperable, and you were in tremendous pain. Your father and I then had to make the worst and hardest decision of our lives... we had to put you down and let you go. That was no way for you to live; you deserved dignity, and that wasn't the life for you.

I truly believe that you took away your brother's pain. His hemorrhage is not dissipating on its own, it's getting smaller because you took it away from him. How could you have had this growth on your spine for so long without showing any signs? How could you have walked and jumped like you did? It doesn't make sense. I think that you knew that this is exactly where I always wanted to be in my life, and you wanted to make sure that I was happy and that your brother could grow up healthy!

For that, I thank you and love you more than words can express!

Thank you for being the best dog ever and sacrificing your life for your brothers!

XOXO,

Mommy

We truly believed that Roxy had taken away Logan's pain and the hemorrhage in his brain. We were confident that when we went back for our follow-up in March, we would continue to receive good news about Logan.

CHAPTER

4

I HAVE LOST count of the number of times I have started writing this chapter. I have a visual of what it would look like if I were using a typewriter instead of typing this on my computer. I can see the wastebasket overflowing with crumpled pieces of paper as my fingers sit frozen atop the keys. Writing about the worst day of my life is crippling. This day is why I have PTSD and trauma, not to mention zero patience for bullshit (we will get to that).

The day Logan was diagnosed with a brain tumor was the worst day of my life. It's the hardest thing to write about and to relive. In all honesty, I've blocked out many of the details from this day. Thankfully, I have many people around me who were willing to share their memories of that day. With the help of my friends and family, I've been able to revisit those events and write this chapter. (And I won't lie, there may have been some wine involved in the writing.)

I had been back to work since February 3, 2017, and we were settling in nicely to being working parents and having Logan at day care. Life was great; it was everything I had always wanted. A close family friend, Kim (aka Aunt Kimmie), was the one who watched Logan while we worked. Monday through Friday I would drop Logan off at Kim's, and Kevin would pick him up.

On Tuesday, March 7, I was the one to pick Logan up. As I was leaving Kim's house, one of the other children whom she watches said, "Bye Logan, we'll see you tomorrow!"

And Kim replied, "Not tomorrow. Logan has a doctor's appointment, but we'll see him later in the week!"

In fact, on March 8, the day of the diagnosis, we had appointments set up for an early intervention program to come and set up occupational and physical therapy for Logan. These appointments were canceled, as was most of the rest of my life for the immediate future. But, for those first three months, we had been living like any other new parents; we were exhausted, overwhelmed, and totally in love with our new son.

I even got to do typical "new mommy" things, like taking Logan for a newborn photography session with my friend, Alice. I had met Alice on Facebook because she was following my #40andknockedup posts. We quickly bonded over our shared sense of humor and salty language. Alice is a nurse by trade, and a professional photographer with a focus on newborn photography. I had shared with her about our early concerns with my pregnancy, and she had been worried for me and Logan. As a nurse, she knew just how many things could go wrong with a pregnancy. A few weeks later, Alice and I had met in person at a baby expo and she offered to take my newborn photos for free. I agreed, and when the photo day arrived, Alice had heated her studio to a cozy eighty-four degrees and had turned on the anti-startle noise machines in preparation for our session.

As she was patiently waiting for our arrival, I called her and said, "Hey, I'm here in your driveway, and don't laugh, but I can't get the car seat out of the car." Of course, she did laugh. (Who wouldn't?)

"No worries," she said. "I'll be right there."

Alice walked out, opened the car door, and grabbed the

seat while depressing the release button. Out came Logan and the car seat. She even spent the next few minutes showing me how to get him in and out of the car. It was such a silly—and yet totally normal—"new mom" moment, and I was grateful Alice had been there with me. We became fast friends, and she continued to be a steadfast support for us through the trying times that lay ahead.

We knew there would be several follow-up doctors' appointments to monitor Logan, and we were figuring everything out. Logan's second follow-up MRI was scheduled for Wednesday, March 8, 2017. We had purposely scheduled the MRI for 8 o'clock that morning because he had to be NPO (nothing by mouth) for at least eight hours prior. Afterward, we had an appointment with Dr. Adamo, Logan's neurosurgeon, at ten to discuss the MRI results. We were confident that the hemorrhage would be gone by now since the last MRI had shown that it was dissipating.

We arrived at the hospital at just about eight. We were always running late (well, any time I was with my husband at least). The MRI went as we had expected—this was the third one Logan had had in his short three months on this earth.

After the MRI, we went up to Dr. Adamo's office and were brought into a room. We sat and waited for the doctor or a

PCA to come and give us what we had expected would be good news so that we could head home. I remember this next moment so clearly. When Dr. Adamo walked into the room, he didn't say a word, he didn't even acknowledge Kevin or me until the nurse had closed the door. He was about to give us the worst news of our lives. He said to us that the hemorrhage was completely gone but there was a large tumor— one-third the size of Logan's head—in its place, and it was malignant. It took me a minute to realize that "malignant" meant "cancer." Our stomachs were instantly in knots, and everything else that came out of his mouth after that point was a blur.

Melissa, one of Logan's nurses, walked us up to an exam room. Kevin was carrying Logan and I was on the phone, giving updates and letting our family know they were keeping us. Once we were back in the room, I asked Dr. Adamo if Ali, the secretary/angel in Dr. Adamo's office (who had previously moved up our MRI appointment and had since become a close friend), could join us. She stayed just to be with us; there simply were no words that could make sense of any of it. There was lots of hustle and bustle to have Logan admitted right away, and I asked Ali if she would stay with us and go up to the PICU floor. Of course, she did.

They immediately admitted Logan to the pediatric intensive care unit (PICU) because they wanted to biopsy the tumor and see what they were fighting. Our baby would be going in for brain surgery the very next day. The gravity of it all hit us like a sledgehammer. In the span of a moment, our family's whole life had been turned upside down. There is no way to adequately explain the emotions that overcome you when you are told that your son needs to be immediately admitted to the hospital. We were beyond terrified. I felt like I was living in a nightmare that was impossible to wake up from. *Brain surgery. On my baby. How was this even possible? What were we going to do? How would Kevin go to work? I can't do this on my own! How could either of us go home without Logan? It's not a home unless we're all there together.* All of these thoughts, and so many more, were flooding my brain. I didn't have any answers, but I had a million and one questions.

When we got upstairs, Logan was given a room, and then everyone started coming in. Kevin stepped into the hall to make a phone call and the nurses came in to place an IV. With tears in my eyes, I asked Ali to stay with Logan because I just couldn't watch. My heart was breaking for my sweet baby. I clearly remembered about a week prior telling Kevin that I had felt like Logan's head had been getting bigger. But I had just kept brushing it off, thinking it was just my mommy brain playing tricks on me, like I was just overreacting and trying to find something wrong. To this day, I kick myself for not bringing him to the hospital a week sooner. But what would that have changed? Maybe a lot, but also maybe nothing. Maybe he wouldn't have had the developmental delays, brain injury, or other issues he has now. Maybe he would. We will truly never know, but it constantly eats away at me.

I remember being asked, "When did Logan first start having seizures?" Kevin and I looked at each other and answered, "He didn't. He never had a seizure." The doctors were surprised with that answer and said that if we would have waited one more week, it would have been too late! Too late...meaning that he wouldn't have survived!

I do think it's important to acknowledge how lucky we were with the help we had. Kevin's parents drove from North Carolina to come to be with us and help us, and his closest friends, Jay and Danny, were some of the first people he turned to for help. My parents were still local, and both (as well as their spouses) were there for support and to be with us at the hardest moments. Kevin's parents took care of everything at home; they dealt with everything from caring for our pets to cooking meals and cleaning. It was a godsend; I don't know what we would have done without those people around us. It is not lost on me how lucky we have been that this was (and, to a large extent, still is) part of our story. The saying "It takes a village to raise a child..." I get it. I really get it now.

The morning after Logan's biopsy, Ali came to the PICU to bring me a coffee on her way to work. The room was dark, Logan was sleeping and hooked up to a bunch of monitors, and I was sitting in a rocking chair, alone with all my thoughts and worries. Ali was a welcome distraction from the storm that was swirling in my mind. We had been talking for a little as Ali stood at Logan's crib when a resident walked in and said the words that would shake me to my core. "So, it's likely a glioblastoma." Ali grabbed a hold of the crib because she thought she was going to collapse. It was clear to her that I didn't understand at first what a "glioblastoma" was or what this meant for Logan. I asked Ali what was wrong, but she told me it was OK and that she would have Dr. Adamo come talk to me.

Soon after, we were all called down to a large conference room off the PICU where we were seated at a huge table.

There were so many of us in the room that we could barely squeeze everyone in. Kevin sat beside me, Colby was across from us, and seated next to her was my mom on one side and Kevin's parents on her other side. My dad was seated at the other end of the table. Jane (whom I had recently become close with, as we had just lost a mutual friend to—wait for it—a glioblastoma), Ali, our social worker, and several other doctors were there as well. We had a room full of support, but Kevin and I were frozen with fear. I sat with my hands in front of me on the table, trying to focus on the solidity of the hard surface in a vain attempt to ground my racing thoughts. Kevin sat there stoically, as he does, trying desperately to not show any emotion, even though the pain and fear behind his eyes could have been visible even to the blind.

And then it was said: the "C" word. Our son, Logan, just three months old, who had never smoked, never did drugs, and never worked in an unsafe place, had cancer...in his brain. When the doctor confirmed that it was a glioblastoma, everyone lost it. We knew it was bad.

Searching for some speck of hope, Kevin asked, "Okay, how do we get this taken care of?"

The doctors replied, saying that a glioblastoma can only be treated with radiation, which is not an option for babies.

Then the conversation turned to palliative care. We had never heard about palliative care for a child; that was what you did for Grandma when hospice was going to come in. We were so numb. *He is only a baby! How is this fair?* Kevin and I felt so lost and confused, and we just kept asking ourselves, *How does this happen? What had we done? How could we have prevented this? Is there any explanation?*

Kevin's mom, who is not usually a very emotional person, was trying to get her husband to put his arms around Kevin, and she ended up getting up and holding Kevin herself. Colby was careful to hide her expression and shot a glance at Jane and Ali, who just shook their heads ever so slightly and fought back tears. I just crumpled, and Kevin, whose eyes betrayed him, sat with tears running down his face. Colby gave me a little nod as if to say, "It's OK, you've got this. We will figure it out."

I quickly gathered myself and asked what we do next, because doing nothing was not an option, nor was letting this bastard tumor win. *So what's next?* The doctors said the biopsy was being sent to Boston, but a blizzard was approaching, which could hold up the process of getting a second opinion.

Colby asked the doctor, in no uncertain terms, what the prognosis was. *How long did we have?* (She later shared with me that what she really wanted to ask was, "Do I have to fucking prepare to curl up with my best friend and make sure she is never alone because they may lose their son?") They said that because it seemed to be a congenital glioblastoma, there was a glimmer of hope.

That was all the push I needed. I immediately went into "let's fix it" mode. I couldn't stand the thought of losing my son, and I said to the doctors, "You take him and you make him better. You do whatever you have to do, because God wouldn't have given me this baby only to take him away from me!" Even as a young child, my mom always said I was very stubborn. I never took no for an answer—never! I was always determined to get what I wanted, and I'd do or say anything to make sure that happened. When I think back, I'm so glad that those traits stayed with me because after Logan's diagnosis, all of that came out in full force to fight for my son.

By the time we all got up from the table, the room felt like it had shrunk to the size of a pinpoint. All I could think about was Logan. Although it had all happened so fast, everything felt like it was running in slow motion. All we could do at that point was pray and remain faithful that Logan would get through this. He had to! *We* had to!

Jane, Ali, and Colby excused themselves and went to

the bathroom. They held it together until they got into the bathroom where Jane crumpled to the floor and just started sobbing. Ali and Colby knelt down with her, and the three of them sat there, crying together. They didn't know how they would be able to go back out and try to be positive when Kevin and I had just been given the worst news. They didn't know how, but they knew they would do it—for us. They wiped their tears, fixed their makeup, and went back out there.

My mom cried, screamed, and yelled at God. *Why? Why Logan? Why her only grandchild? Why God?* She did all of this in private because she wouldn't allow herself to break down in front of me. She felt she had to be strong for me, to let me know that everything was going to be OK. (Now I know where I get my "strong mama" traits.)

Our friends and family were already setting up fundraising to help cover the expenses of what was to come. I wasn't too sure about the idea, but they thought it would be needed, and so my close friend, Melissa, took the lead with setting up a website.

In what seemed like the blink of an eye, our entire world had turned on its axis. This would be the beginning of our new living arrangements. Our house that we had made into a home with our sweet new family was now just a memory as the hospital became our new home.

When I called my friend, Kim (or Aunt Kimmie, as Logan knows her), to tell her the news about Logan's diagnosis, I said with a calm, somber voice, "It's more than water; it's a tumor. He has cancer." I could almost hear her heart drop to the floor as the words left my mouth.

She replied, "How can this be? Yesterday we were just talking about how he had mastered moving the stuffed monkey from one hand to the other! He loves that little stuffed monkey!" And then she said to me with absolute certainty, "He's your kid. He's got this. And I'm here for you to scream when you need to, with no judgment or offense."

I was calm—numb, really—but her words were the strength I needed in that very moment. I said, "He's gonna beat this." I knew deep down that he would, but I was still scared as hell.

Within that very first day, our friends had rallied around us and proved that it truly does "take a village." Without their support, I don't know how Kevin and I could have gotten through that brutal transition of living in the hospital and facing the dreadful uncertainty of our baby's future. My friends, Bridget and Kim, visited and offered much-needed comfort for me (in the form of carbs and alcohol), and for Logan, as they sang to him while he was hooked up to countless tubes and cords. Despite their efforts, Logan was very agitated (who wouldn't be?), and to this day he still gets upset when Bridget sings to him, although now it's for a different reason. ("American Idol" is not calling her.) My friend, Claire, had lived through the NICU nightmare with different circumstances, and she didn't know what to say or how to help, but she prayed for Logan's recovery and for strength for me and Kevin. She also wisely told me that this would be a marathon, not a sprint. And my friend, Lisa, a fellow cancer mom, urged me to take it all minute by minute and day by day.

Inside, my emotions were reeling, and my thoughts were all over the place. *What's going to happen to my baby boy? Will he have to go through chemotherapy? What will that be like for him? What the hell are we in for?! And why—why—was Logan having to endure this?!* It was like there was a storm raging in my head and in my heart. But, on the surface, I did everything I could to stay calm and collected because I knew I had to keep my shit together for Logan.

On March 13, the hospital's pediatric chaplain, Daina, came to Logan's room to perform his baptism. We had gone to our church to pick up the documents needed for the baptismal certificate, and we brought the papers, along with holy water straight from Italy, to the hospital. Colby (my best friend) and Dan (Kevin's best friend) were there as Logan's godparents. We all stood praying over Logan's hospital bed as he lay there with his eyes closed, machines beeping around him, and him squirming every now and again. This memory always strikes me as funny because Colby is not a religious person and she gets super uncomfortable doing religious things, but I never saw her waver. I don't know if she did it for me, or for Logan, or if she just closed her eyes and prayed to not catch on fire, but she *looked* like she was praying with the rest of us! Colby later told me that she had been terrified that we had rushed to do the baptism in case something bad happened during the next surgery. Daina was so sweet too, and she performed the baptism, with all of us crying, with the utmost professionalism and care.

It seems so surreal now—the diagnosis, the questions, the people, all of it. To this day, I can only recall the bare minimum of what happened in those first few days. My brain has protected me from most of it. What I've since learned in therapy is that this is what happens when we experience PTSD from a traumatic event. Our memories are sparse in order to save us. I'm grateful that my subconscious has shielded me from those recollections, and I'm thankful for my friends and family who have held those memories for me all these years. The day Logan was diagnosed with cancer was the beginning of so many twists and turns that would push us all to our limits. And it was also the beginning of a journey that would prove that miracles *do* happen, and even when we are facing the most horrible circumstances, sometimes we are exactly where we're meant to be.

CHAPTER

5

BY THE TIME Logan was born, I had been working at Aflac for five years. And in those early years, I could never have imagined how fate would intervene to create life-saving connections between my professional work and Logan's battle against cancer.

You may recall that my career at Aflac had begun somewhat reluctantly as I had initially turned down the job, only to become an independent benefits consultant a few years later when my life circumstances had changed. I began working for Aflac in May 2011, and I quickly became one of their top agents in the state by the end of that year. I continued to excel and won all sorts of awards, trips, and contests, all while still teaching dance and bartending on Friday and Saturday nights. Things were moving along smoothly. Kevin and I had moved into our own place, and life was good! In March 2014, I badly sprained my ankle while teaching Zumba, and there went my teaching and bartending for several weeks. When I was finally healed and able to go back to bartending, I had been doing so well with Aflac that I no longer needed the additional income, and I decided not to go back to working at the bar. Who knew that a career selling insurance for commission only would work out?! A few months later, I was promoted to coordinator in training (which is just as it sounds—training to become a district sales coordinator). Then, in February 2016, I became a district sales coordinator. I was killing it! I was always in the top five of the coordinators in the state, and I was hitting my quotas and goals, and earning prizes, awards, and trips.

When I found out I was pregnant with Logan in April 2016, I felt like I was on top of the world. I finally had everything I had always wanted—a great husband, an amazing career, financial stability, a home, and now a baby—a boy too! Life was *great*! I even had the financial freedom and career flexibility to be able to stay home with my son for as long as I wanted after he was born.

When Logan was born in November 2016, I added him to my Aflac policies: the accident plan, the hospital plan, and the cancer plan. I also got him a life insurance policy. Thankfully, I did that before he was diagnosed, because based on his current health history, he would not have qualified for life insurance. (Parents—*please* get your children life insurance as early as possible. Don't think about it for the morbidity factor; think of it as a vehicle that will help protect their future and their future families.) Because Logan had spent five days in the NICU, I figured I might as well add him to everything while I was at it. I never thought I would have to use my cancer plan on my son; it was just for the peace of mind, which is exactly why I do my job and why I am good at it!

What most people don't know is that Aflac supports the Aflac Cancer and Blood Disorders Center of Children's Healthcare of Atlanta (CHOA), which is a pediatric cancer and blood disorders program. I had been donating monthly to CHOA since I started my Aflac career, and I've increased my monthly donations every year. I knew nothing about childhood cancer before I started working with Aflac. I don't think I even knew anyone who had experienced childhood cancer; I had only heard about it through the stories from Aflac's children's cancer center, which had always pulled on my heartstrings.

When Logan was first diagnosed with a brain tumor, they sent his biopsy to the three major childhood cancer hospitals on the east coast: Memorial Sloan Kettering in New York City, Dana-Farber/Boston Children's Cancer and Blood Disorders Center in Massachusetts, and Children's Healthcare of Atlanta in Georgia. At that time, all I had heard was "New York City," "Boston," and "Atlanta." I hadn't yet put two and two together to realize that "Atlanta" meant CHOA—the very hospital supported by the company I worked for.

When they got Logan's biopsy back, they determined that he had a congenital glioblastoma. (I once made the mistake of googling "congenital glioblastoma," and I will never do that again. The case study I found was done in the 1980s and it didn't show a good outcome. So, a note to anyone battling cancer: *do not google your diagnosis*. Every case is different, every person's body responds differently, and medicine and science are constantly evolving!)

With this new information, Dr. Weintraub and Dr.

Adamo agreed that they were "cautiously optimistic." When I heard that, I thought, *Let's do this. Let's fight this beast.* The way I describe it is that it's the worst type of brain tumor (a glioblastoma) at the best time in his life (congenital, meaning that he was born with it). What makes it congenital is subjective; it means that he was born with it, but at what age does congenital stop being called that as part of the diagnosis? I also learned that brain tumors are graded rather than staged. Logan's tumor was graded at three and four, meaning that it was very aggressive, fast-growing, and once treated, could come back.

Logan's doctors received different treatment options and diagnosis realities from each of the three hospitals. At the time, there were less than one hundred documented cases of congenital glioblastoma—and that's probably still true to this day. In fact, some say that Logan is only number eighty-seven or eighty-eight. And he was the very first patient that Dr. Weintraub had ever treated with this diagnosis.

The outcomes and plans from Sloan Kettering and Dana-Farber were not very positive, although each cancer diagnosis is different, and everyone reacts differently to treatment plans, chemo, and radiation. But then we received a somewhat hopeful treatment option from CHOA. They had recently had a child with a similar diagnosis and had been successful in treating the tumor. Again, every case is different, but this gave us hope.

One day, within the first week of Logan being diagnosed, I was in the PICU when I received a phone call from Atlanta. Before I even answered the call, I knew it was a Georgia phone number because Aflac's corporate headquarters are located there, and our customer service department is based there as well. I had made and received several calls from there over the years that I'd been with Aflac. Earlier on, I had connected with Jackie Williams, a fellow district sales coordinator and CHOA ambassador for our Aflac market. She had reached out to me and had sent me paperwork to fill out to send to CHOA to have them review Logan's case. And here I was, sitting in the PICU, when I received the call from Atlanta. It was a doctor from CHOA. I began speaking with the doctor while I was flagging down Dr. Weintraub. I told her who I was speaking with and that they said they could help. (Recalling this moment literally makes me tear up and gives me chills because this was an absolute *game changer*!) I was on the phone with the head of the department that Dr. Weintraub had been trying to get a hold of! She asked,

"Is that Dr. Mazewski?" And I said yep, and handed her the phone.

Since CHOA had presented the best outcome and option for treatment, Dr. Weintraub and her team chose that plan. Now, here is another moment that totally convinced me that everything happens for a reason and that this was all meant to happen. I work for Aflac (as an independent benefits consultant), I sell cancer insurance for a living, Aflac helps support CHOA, and CHOA wrote the treatment plan that saved Logan's life. You can't make this shit up! So, once again, I am a firm believer in fate, and I know without a doubt that Logan chose us to be his parents for a reason. Working for an amazing company, being a policyholder, donating to an amazing cause, and then having Logan's chemo protocol come from CHOA is all just so incredible.

Logan's treatment plan consisted of a very aggressive combination of chemotherapy drugs, the names of which I had never heard of, nor could I pronounce any of them. Mind you, according to the St. Baldrick's Foundation, studies have shown that in the past *twenty years* there have only been *two* new drugs specifically developed and approved to treat children with cancer. So the plan that was devised for Logan included drugs that adults would receive. This news was pretty sad and scary! The plan included five rounds of inpatient chemotherapy and eight rounds of maintenance chemo for a total of thirteen rounds and about eighteen to twenty months of treatment in total, depending on how quickly he recovered between rounds.

He started his first round of chemotherapy on Friday, March 17, 2017. I was confused about how they could start on a Friday, as it was the last day of the workweek, and then I quickly reminded myself that this was a hospital and there was no typical workweek involved, especially when it came to saving a life, and an infant's life at that. The "Induction Regimen A," as the paperwork called it, broke down the days and what chemotherapies would be given on each day. Each cycle was to be twenty-one days, and the schedule ran from day zero to day thirty. Depending on how quickly his counts recovered (we are talking about white blood cell production, specifically neutrophils, which are essential to the body's immune system), this would determine when he could start the next round of treatment. They do it this way because chemo doesn't just treat cancer; it also has many horrible side effects. Dr. Weintraub even told us one day, "When Logan becomes a teenager, make sure you *don't* tell him that he may not be able to have children because of his treatment." That was definitely a funny-not-funny moment. We found it funny and positive in the sense that we were talking about him having a "normal" cancer-free future, but at the same time, it was strikingly *not funny* because what parent doesn't want their child to have children and ultimately become a grandparent themselves? All of the chemotherapy drugs Logan would be receiving had side effects such as secondary cancers, allergic reactions, seizures, shortness of breath, imbalance of body fluids, fever, liver damage, bone pain, diarrhea, fatigue, vision and hearing loss, plus many more. Even the drugs he would be given to help raise his counts had side effects!

For the first round of Logan's chemotherapy, they only did 75 percent of the dosing based on the plan because they wanted to see how he would handle it. (Ugh, how the fuck would *you* handle it?!) Because he's my kid, he handled the first round of chemotherapy like a fucking rock star. Me, on the other hand...not so much. I was so sick during the first two weeks living in the hospital with him. Between not sleeping or eating well, not getting fresh air, and just the stress of it all, I came down with a horrible cold and a sinus infection. Luckily, and ironically, my primary care doctor, Dr. Roche, was right across the street, and he prescribed an antibiotic and a nasal spray for me.

Logan's medical team bumped his second round of chemotherapy to the full dosage because he had handled the first round so well. During this time, he spiked a fever and one of his incisions from his shunt surgery got infected. In the first week that Logan was diagnosed, he had had surgery to put in two shunts that would help drain the cerebrospinal fluid (CSF) from his brain, which would help relieve pressure on his brain caused by the large tumor (also known as hydrocephalus). Cerebrospinal fluid is the salt water that surrounds and cushions the brain and spinal cord. Shunts are very common; they are placed surgically in the skull with a drain to another part of the body where the fluid can be absorbed. He had bilateral shunts at this point (meaning one on each side of the back of his head). They typically put shunts on the top of the head, but because that was where Logan's tumor was, they had put it on the back of his head. So, between the increased dosages, a corner of the incision reopening, and his counts being down, unfortunately infection and fever were risks with his compromised immune system.

As I had mentioned earlier, each round of Logan's treatment was twenty-one days. He received three different types of chemo on day one, day two, and day three. He then received a small dose on day eight and again on day fifteen.

During days twenty-one through thirty they would start the next round of chemo, again, depending on when his counts recovered. Logan was fine for the first week of round two, but on day eight, his counts started to drop. Then, on day ten, we noticed that the area around the incision on his belly (from the shunt surgery) was red and swollen. Plus, when they had changed his bandage, they had his port line rubbing on it... *Ugh!* By day eleven, it looked worse, and I had to be a crazy hospital mom and demand an ultrasound after the doctors had gone back and forth on whether to do one. Thankfully, the ultrasound showed that it was just superficial; cellulitis was the official diagnosis. They put him on two different antibiotics and Tylenol when needed.

On day twelve, Logan was in so much pain and had slept pretty much all day. I was heading home that night while my mother stayed with Logan at the hospital. I wasn't feeling right about leaving, but I went anyway. Before I went to bed, I made sure my ringer was up (normally I would turn it off before going to sleep). Thankfully, I had had the foresight to do that, because I got a call at two o'clock in the morning from my mother, who told me that Logan was having trouble breathing. That was the scariest call of my life. Kevin and I immediately drove to the hospital. They had to call a "rapid response" on Logan, which is just one step down from a "code blue." (If you don't know what "code blue" means, it refers to cardiac or respiratory arrest or any other life-threatening medical emergency.) They determined that his breathing difficulty had been a result of the extreme pain he was in. They had to give him morphine, and thankfully, this allowed him to sleep through the night. Kevin went home around three thirty in the morning, and I stayed at the hospital with my mother. Of course, I didn't sleep a wink; I was just watching him to make sure he was breathing. I finally went home around eleven the next morning and got only about two hours of sleep. I was able to get a few more hours of sleep throughout the day, but it definitely wasn't enough. I was completely exhausted. Kevin had gone to the hospital around three o'clock to see how Logan was doing, and every time I was on the phone with him, I could hear Logan crying in the background. My poor baby was in pain, and I wasn't there to help him. Thank God I was able to text Ali, who was still working in Dr. Adamo's office, and she was able to get in touch with the neuro doctor who was on call and ask them to go see Logan. That made me feel better, but I was still a wreck! There is no worse feeling in the world than feeling helpless when your child is in pain. I wanted to go back to the hospital, but I was beyond exhausted, and I knew it would have done no good for Logan or myself.

Here are just a few examples of what I was feeling during this time, some of which I had experienced in the same day: angry, happy, sad, bitter, pissed, upset, blessed, hopeful, defeated, loved, scared, weak, strong, betrayed, lonely, exhausted, alone, afraid, anxious, jealous, confused, hopeless, weary, and brave. I'm sure there were even more, but that gives you an idea.

As much as what we were going through was horrible, and I would not wish it on anyone, I still believed in my heart that Logan was always meant to be here and that we were meant to be his parents and to face this with him. We would never know why or how this was happening, but we were determined that Logan would *always* know *love*! That was all that mattered, and that's still all that matters. And as difficult as it was for our marriage, Kevin and I were committed to *always* support our son and do what was right for him. This was the worst roller-coaster ride I had ever been on. There were days when I just wanted to cry, but I knew that I had to stay strong for our son. I would give Logan pep talks every day, and I swear he understood me. I would say to him, "You've got this," or "Keep fighting, Bubba," or "You're a fighter, a warrior," or "You are strong." I even got to the point where whenever he would sneeze, I would say, "God bless you, Bubba," and I'd imagine him replying, "I know, Mommy. God blesses me every day."

During that time when I was living in the hospital, I was asked numerous times, "What do you do with all your free time?" You would think that not working and basically allowing other people (nurses, patient care assistants [PCAs], etc.) to take care of my son would allow a decent amount of free time... *Not!* That couldn't be further from the truth. There were days when I had no idea where the time went, and then there were days (very few of them) when the time would go by so slowly. I had lots of ambitions and a list of things I wanted to accomplish during my "free time" in the hospital, but that list always just continued to grow, and not many things would get checked off. I can't even describe what a typical day looked like because they were all so very different. My son always came first, so I needed to make sure that he was taken care of before I did anything on my list. The nurses and PCAs checked on him every three or four hours, whether it was for meds, a neuro check, or to check his vitals. Other than that, I was on my own. Logan was also getting physical therapy, occupational therapy, and speech therapy, each at least two or three times a week. He had at least three doctors tending to his care daily, as well as a developmental pediatrician who monitored him on a weekly basis. In addition to all of that, if he had a surgery or anything additional they were monitoring, he had a specific doctor for that checking in daily as well, sometimes more than once a day.

I would try to get out of the hospital for a run or to work out, but I couldn't leave his room if he was awake. Volunteers would sometimes come to sit with him, but I was very cautious and picky about who I would let near him, especially when his counts were down. One of the volunteers, Annabelle, was great with Logan, and she absolutely adored him. She would come in once a day and play with him for about half an hour while I went out for a run. That was typically the most "free time" I ever had. Sometimes I would sneak out when Logan was napping so that I could grab a cup of coffee or just get some fresh air, but during that time, his naps were very sporadic, and I would be lucky if he took a ten- to fifteen-minute power nap a few times a day. So, needless to say, I had to be "on" at all times, hence the exhaustion. Not to mention that I was sleeping on the couch at the hospital, which was not very comfortable, and the nurses would be coming in and out all night for Logan's feeds, meds, neuro checks, vital checks, and diaper changes.

During the week, my mother and my husband would come at night to give me a break and to help with Logan. Although we limited visitors because Logan was immuno-compromised, my dad and a couple of our friends would occasionally visit during the day or would come to take me to lunch or bring me coffee. My mother-in-law also came on the weekends to relieve me. One weekend, when I got home after my mother-in-law came to relieve me, I walked into my house, and as I walked into the dining room and looked straight into the living room, I noticed that my entire living room had been rearranged! *What?!* I immediately called my husband to bitch to him, but not before I moved everything back. I told him he needed to talk to his mother, and when he did, her response was, "Well, if you can't change your life, you change your surroundings." (In this case, my living room.) While I agreed with the sentiment, I said, "Yeah, in your own house." Thankfully, we can joke about it today.

Kevin and I even had an occasional date night on Fridays at our favorite village restaurant, the Mohawk Taproom and Grill. I had to stop "checking in" on Facebook when we went there because the owners would always comp our dinner. We were grateful, but it wasn't necessary. As it turned out, they still knew when we were there because there were cameras, and they still comped our meals. (Thanks, Mike and Stephanie!) I never wanted to do much when I was home on the weekends because I was so exhausted, but I also didn't want to be away from Logan, so even though it was my weekend "off," I would still go to the hospital for a few hours each day.

I really kept to myself while we lived in the hospital, and I usually only chatted with Logan's medical team, the volunteers, and any administrator who needed me to sign another damn paper. I wasn't there to make friends; I was there to protect my son and to save his life! Especially when going through this type of situation, you can't force a friendship. However, there were two cancer moms with whom I did end up becoming close during this time. One was Michelle, with whom I had graduated high school. Her son, Patrick, had been diagnosed with leukemia about five months before Logan's diagnosis. We hadn't been close in school, but she is now like a sister to me; we have a bond like no other.

When I told Michelle I was writing this book, she said, "You better put in that part where you helped me that one day!"

I said, "Of course! I will *never* forget that day..."

Both Logan and Patrick were in inpatient, in the middle of their chemo treatments. I was sitting in Logan's room, and Kevin was with me as I was pumping (Logan received my breast milk throughout his treatment; it had been a goal of mine because something in me told me that he needed Mama's milk to help him get through chemo). As I was pumping, I heard the loudest shriek I had ever heard. In the pediatric wing, it's not uncommon to hear random sounds—screaming, arguing, laughing, and whatever else might be happening—through the hallways at any given time. But this was different. I heard the loud scream again, and I said to Kevin, "Holy shit, that sounds like Michelle!" I immediately stopped pumping, put my bra and shirt back on, and ran out of Logan's room. Michelle was in the hall, screaming for help. Patrick had coded—yes, they called a code blue. No parent ever wants to go through that! I told her it was going to be OK. It was early in the morning, and she had been waiting for her husband to get there so she could go to work. I knew that I had to be calm for her, so I just asked her what she had to do. Who did she need to call? I can't imagine how I would have reacted in that situation. Thank God, they never called a code blue on Logan. I'm not exaggerating when I say there must have been at least a dozen people who ran into

Patrick's room. He was seizing and had stopped responding, which was why they had called the code blue. Thankfully, Patrick was OK and is now almost five years cancer-free and treatment-free. Michelle and I still talk regularly, and she has become such a great friend, a confidant, and a sounding board. There are some things that I can only say to another cancer mom that no one else would understand.

During this time, I had also met another mom named Allie. Her daughter, Aurora, was also fighting a brain tumor. We had connected through our parents because her mother and my father were constantly chatting it up in the Ronald McDonald House hospitality room. This was a room in the hospital that was run by volunteers, where they provided coffee, snacks, lunch, and dinner on certain days of the week. There was also a couch with a TV, and two private rooms with beds and TVs where parents could rest or spend the night. Allie and I didn't really connect much at first because we were both always by our babies' sides. It wasn't until a few weeks later that we would share an experience like no other, which I will share in a later chapter.

Day fourteen was better. Logan finally ate, after not eating for almost three days. He still wasn't eating as much as he normally did, but a little was better than none. Because he hadn't been eating for a few days, his medical team kept suggesting putting in a feeding tube (also known as an NG tube), which I refused each time. *Why would I put a foreign object down my child's throat when his immune system is compromised? Why would I put him through that when I know he doesn't feel well and will eat again in a few days?* The same thing had happened during the first round.

On day fifteen, he got his final dose of chemo for this round. His incision looked worse, but because his counts were going back up, they said it would look worse before it got better since all of the good cells were attacking that location. (He had had to have three platelet transfusions and one blood transfusion during that round.) His incision looked good, then bad, then OK, then worse again.

The emotional roller coaster continued as we waited for Logan's counts to go up, and we were looking ahead to the impending MRI that was scheduled for the following week to see what the tumor looked like. The best-case scenario would be that the tumor had shrunk enough to be removed. The worst-case scenario would be that we'd have to start round three of chemo. We were all hoping for the retraction of the tumor, and I couldn't help but think that my little guy needed a break from chemo!

CHAPTER

6

AFTER LOGAN'S FIRST round of chemotherapy, I had a complete breakdown. I think everything had just finally settled down enough for me to truly feel my emotions and think about what was going on. My five-month-old baby had a brain tumor and was fighting for his life. We weren't able to experience any normalcy with our baby, and I had missed out on all of the "new mom" moments that I had waited my whole life for. *How was this fair? How did this happen? Why him? Why me? Why us?*

To say that the experience was (and still is) a roller-coaster ride would be putting it lightly. Once the doctors had decided on a treatment plan for Logan, it was just go, go, go. Ten days after he was first diagnosed, they had begun treatment, which started with those first two rounds of very aggressive inpatient chemotherapy. Everything had been moving so fast, and I felt like all I could do was tackle one day at a time, one moment at a time.

It was constantly one step forward and two steps back. While the chemotherapy treatment was working, Logan's appetite was suppressed. His mood and energy were also lagging. We knew this would be a long, tough road but we didn't realize just how hard it would be until we were in the thick of things. One day Logan would be happy and alert, and then for the next few days he would be lethargic and tired. He had a constant diaper rash from the chemo, and we had to use gloves to change his diaper. This in itself was devastating—new parents shouldn't have to use gloves to change their baby's diaper because of the toxicity of the chemo in his urine and bowels. My heart would pound at the thought of it, from the heartbreak and anger. He didn't know what was going on; this was just normal to him, and unfortunately, it became normal for us too. To this day, I don't know if—or how—I would be able to handle a "normal" child. There were times when Logan would just sleep all day long and be up all night, or vice versa. Consistent sleep was not an option for me or my husband when we lived in the hospital. Even if Logan slept through the night, his nursing team would be in several times checking his stats, heart rate, temperature, etc. I don't even want to know how much poison my child was actually given in order to beat cancer—it makes me nauseous just thinking about it. But no matter how bad things would get, Kevin and I kept pushing ourselves to stay positive and not think about the worst-case scenarios. Once you go down that rabbit hole, that's what you focus on—and that's what will happen. We are both firm believers that you reap what you sow, and you get what you give. So any time we caught ourselves thinking the worst—and yes, it did sometimes happen, and still does—we forced ourselves to snap out of those negative ideas as quickly as we had thought them.

Even in moments when we had glimmers of good news, I had trouble trusting it. For example, when we were given the go-ahead to bring Logan home after his first round of chemotherapy, I questioned the doctors because I was so scared to take him out of the hospital. By that point, he had been in inpatient treatment for twenty-seven days. He had been diagnosed on March 8, he started chemotherapy on March 17, and now we were being sent home on April 4. (I remember that specific date because it's also my uncle's/god-father's birthday. It's crazy the significance that certain dates can bring to your life when you are going through something like this!) So much had already happened in such a short period of time, and I was worried about being away from the medical team at the hospital. So, when Logan's doctors told us he could go home, I kept asking them, "Are you sure? Is this OK?" They reassured me that Logan's ANC levels had come back quicker than they had expected. (ANC is absolute neutrophil count, and neutrophils are a type of white blood cell that helps to fight infection. Chemotherapy reduces the ANC, and the lower someone's ANC count, the higher their risk for infection will be. *Oh, the many things you learn when your child is going through cancer treatment!*)

Being a mom of a child with cancer is one of the hardest things on the planet. Trying to balance my own pain and fears while still being strong and keeping it together for my son was a constant battle. Most of the time I had to be laser-focused on taking care of Logan, which often meant stuffing my own feelings down because I just couldn't face them in the moment. To save my son, I needed to summon depths of resilience and strength I would have never thought were possible. And that's the thing about being a mom—we do what we have to do to get shit done and be there for our kids—and we usually end up surprising ourselves in the process!

The roller-coaster ride of childhood cancer is filled with ups and downs, yes, but it's also filled with hidden moments and significant meanings. I have always believed in God and in the power of prayer, but if I'm honest, I had let that slip over the years. My faith hadn't wavered, but I had failed to make it a part of my daily practice. I knew that when we had a kid, I would want to have him baptized, and faith would be a part of our kid's upbringing; I just didn't know how much or to what point. When Logan was diagnosed, I turned immediately to prayer, and I realized why it was so important to keep this as a daily practice. Though I'd never wish for this diagnosis for my son (or anyone, for that matter), I can say that it brought me back to my faith and showed me how mighty the healing power of prayer can be.

I've lived my life desperately trying to show strength and positivity. Sometimes this can be looked at as being bitchy or overpowering, but my motto is to "live life like you want it to be." If I had shown the fear or the sadness I was feeling, what good would that do? I've never really cared if someone else doesn't like it because, honestly, they can go somewhere else then. I don't need them in my life. When Logan got sick, it was like I had been preparing for this role my whole life. I didn't have a choice. I *had* to be strong. I *had* to have fortitude. I *had* to keep going. My husband is the strong, silent type. Me? Not so much. I am going to be heard, dammit! I truly feel that this trait is necessary when you're fighting for someone or something. So maybe those years of training myself to focus on the end result, of pushing people when I felt more needed to be done, of questioning things that just felt a bit "off," were all in preparation for the biggest fight of my life.

Kevin and I believe that if God brings you to it, He will bring you through it, *and* that God doesn't give you more than you can handle. No matter how much it might suck, everything does happen for a reason. Logan chose us to be his parents because he knew we would fight for him to the ends of the earth. We feel that we are strong enough for him—and for each other—to get him through this and past this. Not only were we fated to be in Logan's life, but this experience has also proven that God does have a plan for each of us—and people and circumstances come into our lives at just the right times. The fact that I work as an independent benefits consultant with Aflac and sell cancer insurance for a living is one of many ironies we've encountered. Thank God I had added Logan to our cancer plan when he was born (even though I thought we would never have to use it). Without Aflac's children's cancer center, Logan wouldn't have had the chemotherapy treatment plan he had received. I was also a member of the Capital Region Rotary Club that donated toys to the children's hospital at Albany Medical Center every year, and we were recipients of that program during our first year in the hospital. Also, one of the women whom I was in Rotary with was engaged to the general manager at the Hilton hotel across the street from the hospital, and he comped us a room whenever he had availability so that we could get a decent night's rest and still be near Logan. As I said, many ironic things have played out along the way to bring us so much support we couldn't have imagined.

From day one, we were surrounded by a great medical team and a solid network of friends and family. But even with so many helping hands around us, it could still feel so damn lonely. No matter how much empathy people tried to show toward us, I felt like they could never really understand what we were going through. People would constantly offer unsolicited advice. Especially at the beginning of this journey (it still happens now, but not as much), everyone was a fucking "expert." Everyone would tell me what I "should" do, what would "fix" Logan, and what would help my husband and me deal with it. And as much as I appreciated their outpourings of love and concern, they could never know what they would do or how they would feel if they were in our situation—and even then, they'd never really fucking know! (Some people even went so far as to suggest using cannabis to cure Logan's cancer. *Please do your research on this!* I won't even dignify this with a discussion.) It was also suggested to me (and to Kevin) to join a support group. There were a few issues with this. First, being that childhood cancer is so rare, there weren't any local support groups in our area. Second, because Logan's case was so rare, there weren't any specific support groups that focused on his diagnosis. And third, honestly, why would I want to join a support group (specific or not) to sit around a room and take on the emotions and stresses of other cancer parents who were also fighting for their children's lives? Just the thought of it made my heart race. Didn't I have enough of my own emotions to deal with without bringing other people's struggles into the mix?

I was also quickly realizing that the further along we went in this experience, the less bullshit I could tolerate and the smaller my filter was becoming. I no longer had the time or patience for anyone's minor issues. I couldn't stand to hear about anyone's fucking stubbed toe, or how their kid had talked back to them. I had zero patience for other people's failings, and I just didn't have the energy or attention to accommodate people's bullshit. I couldn't understand how, with my plate as full as it was, I could get all my shit done—I returned calls, I handled my responsibilities, and then some—and yet some people couldn't even return a text or would have anxiety over little things. Yes, I know, everyone is different, and I am constantly reminding myself of this. I also now know that you can't expect *you* out of other people. But at the time, I was placing my own standards on other people—and it was further isolating me.

All of the internal struggles I had been facing finally came to a head just before we found out that we were allowed to go home. When I had that complete meltdown, I cried for two days straight! To be honest, I think the tears and the breakdown came from a place of pure fear. I had been in fight mode for almost two months, and now we were getting a break. *A break? What the hell does that mean? A day or two at home and then we're right back to the hospital to continue the fight?!* I was scared shitless that I didn't know how to be a "mom" because all I had known at this point was how to fight. I was beyond exhausted, and I didn't know how I was going to continue at that pace for the next twelve to sixteen months. How the fuck was I supposed to stay strong for that long?

It was gut-wrenching to know that I would be able to come home with my baby but would then have to go right back to the hospital just days later. All of this seemed so surreal, so unfair. This whole fucking journey sucked; it had been the biggest punch in the gut—no, scratch that—punch in the fucking face, you can imagine. I *hated* that our lives had been consumed by cancer, and doctors, and therapists, oh my! But I *love* my son, and I would continue to do anything needed to get him through. When we got home, it was like the rest of the world stopped. It would have been great to be able to lay in bed with my baby and just cry, but I didn't have that luxury. We were on alert all the time. It was constant checks. Check the port, check the incision, check his breathing, check his temperature. Check, check, check, check, breathe. Check, check, check, check...it was exhausting and terrifying, but it just *was*. That was our life. And, honestly, I was on autopilot at that point. A meltdown was a luxury I didn't have time for.

I'm the type of person who isn't afraid to ask for help or advice, but it has to be on my terms and on my timeline. I can recognize when I need to ask for help, and I won't reach out any sooner than that. So, after my breakdown, I called Dr. Weintraub's office first thing that Monday morning, and I reached out to the social worker, Courtney. I was ready to talk, and I just needed someone to tell me it was going to be OK. I met with Courtney and Dr. Weintraub, and when they asked me what my biggest concern was, I said bluntly, "I don't want my son to die!" I had been so strong and confident up until then, but I felt like I couldn't handle it anymore. They said this was all normal and that I would probably always feel this way. (*Thanks for the fucking pep talk!*) But they were still "cautiously optimistic;" Logan had been doing so well, and they weren't concerned. If only I could have felt the same way! The thing was, I didn't *want* to feel scared or have negative thoughts. Again, I firmly believe that what you think about is what you attract, and I believe that thoughts become things, but I couldn't get that negativity out of my head. Even to this day, I sometimes struggle with this, and it sucks! My husband has always been absolutely amazing and so supportive. Any time I get upset or mention that I'm feeling this way, he turns it around and tells me that Logan is going to be fine. He, too, believes that you get what you put out there.

I am generally a very open person, and I think that is one of the reasons why I have chosen to be so open in sharing

Logan's fight and our story (with my husband's permission, of course). From the very beginning, I was not shy about asking for help in the form of prayers and positive thoughts. I have never believed more in the power of prayer than I have since going through this journey. On the day we found out that Logan had a congenital glioblastoma and that the doctors had no hope, I posted on Facebook and asked for prayers. Two days later, the doctors told us they were confident with the treatment plan they had received and were now "cautiously optimistic." Since then, any time I've posted on social media asking for prayers, everyone has come through. When I asked for prayers for Logan's counts to go back up, they went up so quickly that we were allowed to go home for a few days. I would share Logan's progress daily on Facebook (he had his own Facebook page that a friend created to help us keep everyone updated). I shared the good, the bad, and the ugly. I shared the truth of what we were going through, and I continue to do so. From the first day he was admitted into the PICU, I posted on Facebook that they needed to run more tests and that we needed prayers. That first day, they told us he wasn't going to survive, then three days later they were cautiously optimistic. There will never be anyone who can convince me that people's prayers for our son didn't help this to happen as well.

So much had happened in that first month since Logan's diagnosis and treatment. My husband had to go back to work, and my father-in-law had to go back to North Carolina, which left just my mother-in-law and me to tag team all of the hospital duties. My mother and father both worked full-time and helped as much as they could. My friends, Dani, Colby, and Ali (my angel), put on a successful fundraiser for our family. And we were all just trying to find our way together and fight for Logan.

At the same time, we also knew we needed to bring awareness to the issue of pediatric cancer and the lack of funding for finding a cure. Did you know that only 4 percent of federal funding goes toward children's cancer research? More money is spent on research for adult cancers that could be preventable by life choices, and not that those aren't important as well, but what about our children being our future? If there was more funding for children's cancer research, maybe one of the kids who would be saved could find a cure for cancer! Even as we were in the thick of it with Logan's own fight, we were already thinking about how we could play a part in helping other kids who were also battling cancer.

CHAPTER

7

"Announcing the Logan Strong™ Foundation—Jennifer, Kevin, and Logan Fogg are thrilled to share with you the establishment of the Logan Strong Foundation. The foundation's purpose is to help raise childhood cancer awareness, and to provide items of comfort and support for children and families while they are fighting cancer in and out of the hospital."

YEP, WE DID it...in January 2018, we started a foundation. We had been blessed with so much help from many local organizations that had helped guide us and ease our stresses and pains throughout our journey. And even in the middle of Logan's treatment, we knew we wanted to start a nonprofit that would be aimed at giving back to our fellow cancer families. In honor of Logan's amazing fortitude and strength in fighting cancer, we decided to name it the "Logan Strong Foundation."

I grew up with a strong appreciation for the support that nonprofit and volunteer organizations provide to their communities. Rotary International (the world's largest volunteer organization) has always been an important cause for my family. My father is a past club president, and as a summer youth exchange student myself, I volunteered for all kinds of service projects like singing at nursing homes, working at pancake breakfast fundraisers, and doing highway clean-up days. In middle school and high school, I joined the Key Club (a volunteer organization) and the Builders Club (a student-led community service organization). Then, while in college, I taught dance to inner-city kids. Later, in my thirties, I decided to join Rotary myself. As it turned out, I couldn't find a Rotary club that I resonated with, so I chartered a new one! Giving back and volunteering is in my blood—it's who I am; it's what I do. So starting our own foundation felt like just a natural progression in our journey!

While many amazing local organizations had helped us while we were living in the hospital, we felt there were some gaps that we could help fill. We were fortunate not to have any serious financial concerns during Logan's treatment, thanks to help from my residual income and our Aflac policies. However, money isn't the only thing that you worry about when your family is battling childhood cancer. Yes, I said "family." What many people don't realize is that when a child is diagnosed with cancer, the whole family—and then some—is affected: mom, dad, siblings, grandparents, aunts, uncles, friends, coworkers, etc. In our case, it was primarily Kevin and me, Kevin's parents, my dad and his wife, and my mother and her husband who were most directly impacted. And as we came to find out first-hand, a childhood cancer diagnosis affects each member of the family differently. We, as a family, realized that the best way to help with that would be to not only provide items of comfort and support but to also empower our fellow cancer families to fight, raise awareness, and fundraise for their own families too.

As we were developing the Logan Strong Foundation, we decided that the logo should not only represent Logan and childhood cancer but also our goal to "smack the *puck* out of cancer." As you might remember, my husband is a huge hockey fan and he played hockey as well. Plus, hockey was really the basis of how Kevin and I had first met. We had met while watching hockey at a bar, and our first date was at a hockey game. At the time, I was a New Jersey Devils fan and he was a New York Rangers fan. When our friend started the

LoganStrong.org website for us to share Logan's journey and for people to donate funds to our family, there were three options to donate. The first option was for Rangers fans, the second option was for Devils fans, and the third option was for those who weren't hockey fans! So, as you can imagine, the logo for the Logan Strong Foundation had a gold and gray ribbon (gold for childhood cancer awareness and gray for brain tumor awareness), as well as two hockey sticks behind it. This tied together with our love for hockey and how the sport had helped us through Logan's journey.

We officially launched the Logan Strong Foundation with a ribbon-cutting ceremony and our inaugural golf tournament fundraiser in May 2018, followed by a networking cocktail hour and dinner for those who wanted to support the foundation's efforts without taking part in the golfing. We partnered with many local businesses for the event, and we saw an incredible response from the community. We netted over $30,000, which is unheard of for a first-year event. Thanks to those funds, in that first year we were able to provide support for cancer families in so many ways.

We distributed signs that said, *"No touching—your germs are too big for me."* I first came across these signs on Etsy during Logan's treatment, and I personally think every cancer family needs one of these. This sign was so important for us when Logan was going through treatment because everyone had wanted to hold him or pinch his cheeks. But when a child (or anyone) is going through cancer treatment, chemotherapy, radiation, and some of the additional medications will cause their immune system to be compromised (which is also known as being immunocompromised). There were several times throughout Logan's treatment when he was also on precautions, which meant that anyone who entered his room had to be fully gowned with gloves and a mask because he was at such a high risk for infection at that time. Through the Logan Strong Foundation, we purchased these signs in bulk and put them in comfort bags that were given to families upon diagnosis. We now also bring them to events where we can share them with families, and we put them in the free box at the Melodies Center when kiddos are going in for treatment. They are now a staple item that the foundation provides.

The Melodies Center at Albany Medical Center is where children receive their outpatient chemotherapy. There is a waiting room, a small playroom, and a smaller computer and games room where families can pass the time. They are in constant need of support to help replace items in these rooms, not only due to heavy usage but also for cleanliness purposes, and the Logan Strong Foundation has been proud to fulfill their wish list for those supplies.

My personal favorite comfort item that we continue to provide to this day is called "Ocho." When Logan was going through treatment, someone had gifted him a crocheted octopus. These are typically made for babies in the NICU because the tentacles of the octopus represent the umbilical cord, providing comfort for the baby. It's another item I think every cancer family should have because it's so comforting and relaxing for the baby to just grab and rub the tentacles. Being the "creative" person I am, I one day started calling this octopus "Ocho," and the name just stuck. (For those who may not know, *ocho* means *eight* in Spanish.) Ochos are hard to come by, so we initially had to put out requests on social media for our crochet friends to make them, and we had volunteers drop them at the local American Cancer Society HopeClub. My best friend, Colby, now also makes them and has rallied more people to help from time to time as well.

In the foundation's first year we also donated $1,000 to the Massry Family Children's Emergency Center at Albany Med. Not only is Albany Med one of the largest teaching hospitals in New York state, but it is also one of the leading pediatric hospitals in the Northeast. They pioneered the Massry Center, the region's only stand-alone pediatric emergency center, which provides a safe and special environment where children (up to age eighteen, and sometimes even twenty-one) can be treated by local experts in emergency medicine. They have private rooms, on-site X-rays, child-sized equipment, valet parking, ease of access for ambulances, and so much more. To be able to help on the ground floor of this initiative was a gift. This was important for the Logan Strong Foundation to support for several reasons. First, over 50 percent of pediatric cancer diagnoses start in the emergency room, and when a child has an emergency, the last thing a parent wants to do is bring them to an emergency room where there may be a gunshot or domestic violence victim, drug addicts, overdoses, or the mentally ill. A child does not need to be subjected to that. Also, when a child is going through cancer treatment, you need a one-stop-shop to bring them to because you do not want them to be exposed to more opportunities for infection. The pediatric emergency department helps so many families at all different levels of treatment.

Another one of my favorites from our earliest initiatives was the charging stations we had set up for families. This is a detail that is often overlooked, and yet it can cause so many challenges for families, especially when they need to communicate with their loved ones while their child is in the hospital. On the day Logan was diagnosed, my husband had to run across the street to CVS to buy phone chargers for us. We hadn't known how long we would be at the hospital, and we had only prepared for a trip to the doctors, not a month-long stay. This is the case for lots of families, and so we have installed three cell phone charging stations at Albany Med—one in the pediatric emergency department, one in the Melodies Center, and another in the waiting room of the children's hospital.

Something that is unique to the Logan Strong Foundation is our T-shirts and bracelets. While many organizations and businesses provide these types of sponsored items, we not only offer them to our families, but we also encourage and empower the families to use them for their own fundraising and awareness efforts. During Logan's treatment, we used these items to raise awareness about childhood cancer, and the fundraising piece was also a bonus. We had T-shirts made for each part of his journey. For example, we did T-shirts when he was first diagnosed, with the Logan Strong logo on the front left chest and "We are all #LoganStrong" on the back, with his website for people to either donate or read my blog posts to learn more about our journey. Our second round of T-shirts had the Logan Strong logo on the front left chest, and for the back, my friend created an amazing graphic of a hockey stick smacking a puck, with the words "Smack the Puck out of Cancer." Later, our third round of T-shirts said, "Logan Smacked the Puck out of Cancer," along with the dates when he had been diagnosed and when his port was removed. Someone also donated simple gray bracelets with blue writing that said "#LoganStrong" and "LoganStrong. org," which we now share whenever possible. With these items, the idea is to help other families tell their stories and raise awareness and support from their own communities.

From the beginning, we've also donated gift cards that are distributed to families at the Melodies Center. This program has evolved over the years and will continue to grow as the need arises. Whenever we receive a family application from the Melodies Center at Albany Med, we send them two gift cards for that family—one for groceries and one for gas— along with a brochure about the Logan Strong Foundation and our services, and two letters—one from our family out- reach coordinator and another from me (not as the presi- dent of the foundation, but as a fellow cancer parent). These gift cards could be as little as five dollars, upward to twenty dollars, or sometimes even fifty or one hundred dollars. The point is to provide families with a meal, a cup of coffee, or a treat for them or their child(ren). Every little bit helps! We also donate to families through Amazon wish lists. When a family fills out an application, they also create a list based on their needs or desires, and we purchase those items and ship them directly to the family. It could be clothes, toys, toiletries, furniture, electronics—it is up to the family what to put on their list. We have provided additional support to some of our kiddos with this wish list as well. For example, we had a young lady who needed to go to a hospital in New York City for an extended period to receive her inpatient treatment. We decided to put items together to help make her hospital room more comfortable. We sent a comforter, lights, a charger, pajamas, etc., and this helped her feel so much more at ease while she was in the hospital and away from home for that time.

Another great initiative we have provided is housecleaning services for our families. One of our board members—and one of my closest friends—owns a local cleaning company. When we were going through treatment with Logan, she had donated her time and services to clean our home when we knew we would be coming home from the hospital. We understand the importance of keeping everything clean when a child is going through treatment and they are immunocompromised, and we feel this is a special type of support we can give to families.

While many people know about the Ronald McDonald House Charities (RMHC), which provides a home away from home for children receiving treatment at nearby hospitals (and their families), Krantz Cottage is the first family retreat belonging to RMHC. It is a two-story cottage house in the heart of Lake George, New York. The Logan Strong Foundation supports the RMHC of the Capital Region, where some of our kiddos stay while they are receiving their cancer treatments at Albany Med. We donate items, we volunteer to cook meals, and we support their fundraisers. When we first learned of Krantz Cottage, we immediately knew we had to be a part of it. This was another opportunity for us to get in on the ground floor of a hugely important project for families. As a board, we decided to sponsor the dining room at the cottage, and we were even able to take part in their ribbon-cutting ceremony.

Today, the Logan Strong Foundation is still evolving and recreating itself as we navigate what works, what doesn't work, and what our local childhood cancer families need. Creating and building the foundation has meant so much to my family, and we are always looking for new ways to continue to help our fellow cancer families. We're so grateful for all the support we've received throughout Logan's journey, and this is our way of giving back and bringing that goodwill full circle.

To learn more about the Logan Strong Foundation, please visit our website at https://LoganStrongFoundation.org/.

CHAPTER

8

AFTER THE HEARTACHE of going through Logan's first round of chemotherapy, I couldn't believe we were allowed to go home for a couple of weeks. I was scared and in shock. But I was also grateful that we could finally just enjoy spending time at home with our baby. While at home, we were very protective of Logan. No one was able to visit, other than a few family members and friends (who have always been like family to us). Aunt Kimmy even came over and took some cute Easter pictures of Logan in a suit and fedora! We made everyone wash their hands and use hand sanitizer before even coming near Logan, and if they weren't feeling well, they just weren't allowed to come over.

Then, at the beginning of Logan's second round of chemo, on April 25, around eleven o'clock at night, Logan stopped tracking, which meant he was in a trance-like state and his eyes weren't following. I had known for a few days prior that there had been something wrong with his shunts, but we had needed to get through round two of chemo. After finding out that Logan was not tracking, his doctors did an emergency CT scan and shunt series X-rays later that evening. They also hooked him up to an EEG machine to see if he was having seizures.

Then, around four the next morning, they tapped (or drained) his shunts bedside to release about thirty cc's of CSF, and he immediately went back to tracking. This was how they knew he had been in shunt failure. It was like a Catch-22; the chemo was working, but the particles from the tumor were causing the tubes from his shunts to back up and stop draining.

Around seven o'clock that night, they brought Logan into the operating room to remove his shunts. They tested his CSF again and sent his shunt tubing out for testing to see if there was an infection. Luckily, neither the shunts nor his CSF were infected. However, Logan had an incision on his belly from the initial shunt placement, and this had become infected. The doctors determined that if we waited any longer to remove the shunts, in a day or two we would be able to see the tubing through the infection on his belly— *awful!* (As we eventually found out, his belly was not healing very well because the antibiotic was not working properly. This was resolved once the Infectious Disease department narrowed down what antibiotic to use.)

That same day, Logan was given external shunts and was in the PICU, where he would need to stay as long as his shunts were externalized. They were initially going to reinternalize his shunts the previous Thursday, but after Dr. Adamo (his pediatric neurosurgeon) and Dr. Weintraub (his pediatric hematologist/oncologist) had spoken, they had decided to hold off on that because with Logan's upcoming partial tumor resection, it was best that the shunts remained external while they attempted to remove part (if not all) of the tumor.

After the doctors had decided on surgery and had gone over the risks with Kevin and me, I was an emotional wreck and I felt sick to my stomach. Now, don't get me wrong, this had always been the plan: two rounds of chemo, a surgery to resect the tumor, and then three more rounds of chemo. But this was the most scared that I had been since the day Logan was diagnosed. The chemo had shrunk the tumor significantly, but it was still pretty large for a baby his size. Plus, congenital glioblastomas are very aggressive and very vascular, which means that they move fast and bleed—a lot. Some cases show that partial removal followed by more chemo has had good results in attacking this type of tumor, and Kevin and I had the utmost trust and respect for Logan's doctors, but again, this was all very scary.

One of the biggest risks was that Logan could bleed out uncontrollably and not make it off the operating table. Also, the tumor was pushing on Logan's left frontal lobe, and they weren't sure if it was just pressing on it or if it had actually invaded that area. Either way, he could come out of surgery not being able to use the right side of his body. Whether this could be permanent or temporary, we wouldn't know. It could last a few weeks, a few months, or forever. The good news was that if the latter occurred, since Logan was a baby and his brain was still developing, there would be a greater chance that he would recover, meaning that his brain would grow and would compensate for the parts that had been damaged. If he were an adult, we would be screwed! Logan's developmental pediatrician, Dr. Lucas, was very happy with how Logan had been doing and he said that at the moment, Logan was neurologically sound. Dr. Lucas was confident we would be able to overcome the second outcome if it were to happen.

So, needless to say, I was a hot mess. But at the same time, I was desperately trying to stay positive. The doctors had been telling us worst-case scenarios since the day Logan was born, and he had overcome and proven them wrong every single time. However, even the thought of losing my son was killing me. *Please, God, save my baby.* This plea was on a loop in my head. I did, however, find peace in knowing that Logan was with us for a reason, and I knew we would fight for him no matter what. We had the best doctors, family, support, and prayer warriors we could ever ask for. With that being said, Kevin and I were having final conversations with Dr. Adamo and Dr. Weintraub the following Monday to discuss the surgery.

This all sounds like it was very streamlined, but in reality, *everything* was a hot mess—not just me. It felt like there was a new decision to be made or something unexpected to tackle at every turn. Logan always prevailed, and he always went above and beyond what the doctors expected, but when could we just be faced with a decision about something mundane? When could we stop having to make—quite literally—life or death decisions? And what would happen if we weren't so vigilant? For example, I knew that the infection in his belly had been getting worse due to the placement of the port and where they kept putting the tape. But if I had listened to everyone else and ignored my mother's intuition, they would have continued placing that tape in the same spot, which would have further irritated it, and who knows what would have happened? And what if we hadn't pulled the nurse in to show her that Logan wasn't tracking that night? What would have happened? I felt like I couldn't even blink because I was afraid I would miss something that could save my son's life. All the doctors and nurses were working so hard, but they couldn't possibly catch everything, so we had to.

When Logan was first diagnosed, the tumor had been too large for him to have surgery. We were now at the point where it had shrunk enough that they could go in. The protocols that Dr. Weintraub had read had all stated that we had no time to sit around and wait; they had to go in and remove this tumor as quickly as possible due to its aggressiveness. Initially, I had felt that Dr. Weintraub was strong-arming Dr.

Adamo into doing the surgery. But eventually I was able to step back and recognize that this had likely been my mom brain not wanting my kid to undergo surgery. I ultimately recognized that Dr. Adamo was a professional and would have been completely capable of saying no if he had thought the surgery was not a good idea.

Logan's first resection surgery was on May 9. Thankfully, nothing more had happened between the shunt failure and the surgery. The day of surgery came, and one of the hardest things I have ever had to do was to kiss my baby goodbye as he was prepped for brain surgery. I can't even put into words the feelings that I was having; the only way I can describe it is pure terror. I had faith in the doctors, and I knew we were in the best hands, but it didn't matter. This was my baby, and they were taking out part of his brain. *Please, God, save my baby.* On a loop—yet again.

While Logan was in surgery, we sat in the waiting room, and with us were several of our closest friends and our parents. It was all surreal. One friend was sitting there, typing away and doing work, while other friends were laughing and telling stories to pass the time, and my dad was asking everyone for lunch orders. But we were all just trying not to break down and cry. My child was in surgery. He was having part of his brain removed. I looked at Kevin and we both just gave each other blank stares. We didn't know how to act, what to feel, or what to say.

In this hospital, they would give you a code to watch for updates on the electronic board. It would tell you if the patient was in pre-op, surgery, or post-op. I don't think I ever looked away from that board—for more than eight hours. When I finally saw Logan's status change from "surgery" to "post-op," my stomach dropped through the floor. *Did he make it? Was he OK? Was he going to be able to move?* I didn't care; I just wanted him to be alive. *Please, God, save my baby.*

I stared at the doorway where I knew Dr. Adamo would be coming in. I had a picture in my head of what his face would look like depending on each scenario. When he finally walked through that door, I couldn't read a thing from his expression. He asked us to all go into a private room, and I kept telling myself that this was not for any bad reason; he just wanted to have a private, quiet space. *Tell me!* I couldn't stand it. He said, "We were able to resect 50 percent of the tumor." We all cried. Logan was OK—for now. We could see him shortly.

But what did that mean? It meant that Dr. Adamo wanted to go in again, in a week. *What are you, a fuckin' cowboy?* I thought. I legitimately wanted to go buy him a hat. Two brain surgeries in a week?! Who did he think he was?! Let's just get through this one! But Dr. Adamo said that he now knew what the tumor looked like and how it was acting, and he felt confident about going back in. He was so confident that he felt he could likely go in and get most of the rest of the tumor. *That's wonderful...but can I see my fuckin' kid?* We all cried happy tears, but we knew this moment was fleeting. We knew there was more to come, but we didn't know exactly what we would be facing—and *that* was scary.

When I first saw Logan with his head wrapped like a tiny mummy, all I could think was, *How is that my baby? Does he hurt? How can I protect him from this?* I never wanted to leave his side again. Ever. But overall, my overwhelming feeling was one of gratitude. He was awake, he was alert, and he was moving. My baby was alive and with us! Logan had three external ventricle drains (EVDs) to help the fluid drain from his brain. I mention this because this was the first time—ever—that any patient at Albany Medical Center had had three EVDs. So, why not have my kid be the first one? He was going to leave his mark, one way or another!

At that point, we couldn't think too much about the intricacies that brain surgery on an infant must require because we would drive ourselves nuts (well, more nuts). There wasn't much time to think about anything anyway. Well, there wasn't much time, but there was too much time, all at once. To say this was a confusing time is putting it mildly. At every turn, we had to make a new decision, or comfort Logan, or talk to a doctor, or update a new nurse. But then there were the nights when all you could hear were the beeps of the machines and the cries of other babies, some of whom had no parents there with them. It's hard to tell which is louder, the beeping of the machines or your child crying. Those hours were the longest hours of my life.

After the surgery, we had to worry about swelling on his brain, infection, seizures, and a multitude of other things that we have since buried from our memories in order to maintain some of our sanity. These are the kinds of everyday worries that only fellow cancer families can even begin to understand. One of the amazing things about being a pediatric cancer parent is the community you become a part of. It is a group of amazing people that you never want to be a part of, but you are so thankful it's there. These are the only people in the world who really "get it." However, due to the rarity of Logan's diagnosis, even they couldn't fully comprehend what we were going through. Nevertheless, we made connections in the hospital faster than anywhere I've ever been. I became close with Allie, whose mom had befriended my dad in the Ronald McDonald House hospitality room. Her daughter, Aurora (Rory), also had cancer and was in the PICU. Allie and I would text each other regularly to keep each other updated, show support, and share love and prayers.

In the middle of the night on May 14, we were woken up by a phone call telling us that Logan had been seizing for quite some time. He would stop and then go right back to seizing. They told us that it *looked* like he was seizing, but they could not say with certainty that he was having seizures until they did a CT scan. They had called Logan's neurologist at home, and he was coming in in the morning to look at everything. Until then, Logan continued to be heavily medicated and was watched like a hawk. The CT scan ultimately showed no seizure activity, which was both a relief and also super confusing.

Eventually, the doctors had an answer: chorea. *Uh, WTF is that?* Logan had recently begun kicking his right leg, which we had initially thought was a good sign; the tumor was on the left side, and the left side controls the right, so it was a positive sign that he was moving his right leg. *Yay!* But it wasn't time for a victory lap yet. As it turned out, his kicking was actually an indication of chorea, a neurological disorder that is marked by jerky movements. This was a result of his brain surgery, and the doctors didn't know if it would last forever, or if it would go away with time and with all of the therapies that would be in his future. (What we found interesting was that the word "chorea" is derived from the Greek word for "dance," and I have danced my whole life and taught dance for much of my adult life. See? There were bigger plans at play, and Logan was always meant to be ours!)

On top of everything else, another concern I had—which may be something others wouldn't have thought of with an infant—was an addiction. Logan was on all this medication, and we had to just keep giving it to him. How would this not cause addiction? I asked the doctors if I should spread out his pain meds because weaning him off addictive opioids was the last thing this kid needed. They told me that would be the worst thing for me to do because chasing pain (as opposed to getting ahead of it) was not a place we'd want to be in. This made sense, but with a family history of addiction, the worry never fully left me. Then again, I'm a mom, and I guess worrying just comes with the territory.

During that week of healing, Logan thankfully had no other hiccups except the chorea episodes. We were grateful for his gradual recovery, and we were finding again and again just how necessary it was to be able to ask for help, even though it still doesn't come naturally to me. We had so much help at every turn. Logan was visited by family and friends, and Kevin and I were able to stay at the hotel—which was attached to the hospital—for a couple of weeks. We were given a discount from the hotel that allowed us to do this, and that was a lifesaver in itself. I had been living in Logan's hospital room for so long that I had almost forgotten how to shower because bathing in a sink had become my norm. Wednesdays at the hospital became my favorite day of the week because they had turkey sandwiches for lunch, and when I tell you that these sandwiches were amazing...it's the little things, right?

May 17, the day of the second surgery, had arrived. Dr. Adamo had waited one week from the first surgery—enough time to let Logan's brain heal and not be as swollen, but not long enough to let the little bastard tumor grow. The thought of this was, for lack of a better word, terrifying. We had just gotten through brain surgery—*brain surgery*—on our infant son. And now we had to do it again? We knew that not doing the surgery wasn't an option, but the thought of Logan's little brain being operated on again was almost too much to bear.

In the waiting room, the usual gang was there. And just like a week earlier, we all sat there, staring at the status board, waiting for any hope of good news. Some of us waited patiently, and some of us waited...not-so-patiently. At one point, the social worker (whom we had come to rely on) came in and said, "I just saw inside your kid's head!" Albany Med is a teaching hospital, so anyone can watch the surgery if they choose to do so—we could, too, if we had wanted to. But that was a big fucking no for me, thanks! The thoughts that went through my mind were exactly what you might expect you'd be thinking if your kid was having his brain operated on: *Please, God, let my kid be OK. If the chorea is worse, it's OK! We'll deal with it! Please, God, let my fucking kid live! It's Wednesday...I wonder if my dad will go to the cafeteria and get me a turkey sandwich.* You know—the normal things.

While I was worried and stressed as we waited for Logan to come out of surgery, I was also feeling the same for my fellow cancer mom, Allie. As we were getting positive updates during Logan's surgery, she was receiving not-so-great news about her daughter. During Logan's surgery, I got a text from her saying that she had been given the news that it was not looking good for her daughter. In that moment, I couldn't focus on what she had just told me because I knew it would consume my mind, and I needed to be present for Logan. But then again, how could I not focus on it? Her child was actively dying. That could have been my child.

I couldn't even imagine the pain she must have been feeling. Rory's prognosis wasn't good. She had been misdiagnosed for several months at another hospital before beginning the proper treatment at Albany Med. Allie was doing all she could to stay strong and to fight. Unfortunately, they had moved Rory to the Brave Will Foundation room, a special room in the children's hospital designed to help make families feel more comfortable when their child is passing away.

Rory passed away a couple of days later. I remember passing Allie and Aurora's father in the hallway as they were leaving the hospital for the final time. All I could do was hug her. I didn't know what to say. I'd never told anyone this because it is such a difficult thing to wrap my head around, and honestly, I was ashamed of the thought. I thought it made me a horrible person. And to be honest, part of me was jealous. *Yep, I said it.* I was jealous that her daughter had passed away. Not because she was no longer with her mother and her family, but because she was no longer in pain, and because Allie didn't have to fight anymore. Although I can't even begin to imagine the next fight Allie had to face without her daughter. This is what childhood cancer does; it exhausts you mentally, physically, and emotionally. (Fast forward to a few years later, and Allie is now the mother of two sweet little ones—a girl and a boy—and we still stay in touch. *Cancer moms for life!* These are the bonds that will never be broken! I love you, Allie!)

When Logan's surgery was finally over, I felt like I knew what to look for on Dr. Adamo's face this time. His stone-faced expression wasn't going to fool me. This time I would read it on him. But when he walked through the doors of the waiting room, his face was totally unreadable. *Goddamn, he has perfected that fucking look!* He pointed us to the room where we all squeezed in, some of us sitting on each other's laps, all waiting on two words: "He's OK." What Dr. Adamo told us was that not only was Logan OK, but they were able to remove another 45 percent of his tumor! That meant that, in total, they had removed 95 percent of this tumor that had tried to steal my son from me. Dr. Adamo explained to us that the reason he had left 5 percent of it was that that portion of the tumor was at the midline of Logan's brain (known as the vermis), and he did not want to cross from one half of Logan's brain into the other, to protect Logan's posture and locomotion.

At this point, we were moving into round three of chemo, and I had still been feeling so many different emotions. It had been just about three months since Logan's diagnosis and since our lives had been turned upside down. On one hand, I couldn't believe it had already been three months. But on the other hand, I couldn't believe it had *only* been three months. I can say with certainty that this was *not* at all what we had expected when we were planning for a baby. But I still believe, then and now, that this was meant to happen to us, and that Logan chose us for a reason. Don't get me wrong, this life *sucks big time*, but it is what it is, and you just push forward. There were days when I would just stand in the shower and cry and beg for his pain to go away and for him to be healed. Then I would pick myself back up and keep going.

His third round of chemo was the toughest so far. My in-laws had been helping so much (and we were so grateful), but they had to go back to North Carolina for a week. They had been with us since Logan was first diagnosed. So, for one week, it was pretty much my husband and me. My mom helped a bit, and so did my dad, but it just felt lonelier, like there was more weight on our shoulders than normal. I mean, what the hell was *normal*, anyway?! But not having my mother-in-law around was tough because she had helped me with the laundry and the meals. Plus, Kevin had gone back to work full-time so it was really just me for about twenty hours a day. Don't get me wrong, I wouldn't have wanted to be anywhere else, but it was very tough! The four walls of a hospital room close in on you, and there are only so many "extracurricular" activities one can do. I would sit next to Logan's crib while he slept, or just rest as he slept on me. I would play with him, sit him up, and move his arms and legs. He also had physical therapy, occupational therapy, and speech therapy daily, as well as different doctors coming in at different times during the day. I couldn't work (I tried), it was hard to read or listen to a book, and I couldn't focus on anything other than him. I remember typing my blog posts as he was sleeping or getting a blood transfusion.

I had never seen a baby dry heave or spit up bile, and seeing it happen to my own child was awful. This third round of chemo had been harsher on Logan for a couple of reasons. First, he was coming off of two major brain surgeries *and* this was the third round of poison he was getting. I have to say, though, that my kid is A-M-A-Z-I-N-G! He rarely screamed or cried uncontrollably. He would just fuss or moan to indicate that he was uncomfortable. Thank God he has always been calm-natured like my husband. Don't get me wrong, though, he will tell you exactly like it is—just like his mama!

Speaking of telling it like it is... When Logan was first diagnosed on March 8, my phone was blowing up with texts and Facebook messages. I was very overwhelmed, albeit *gratefully* overwhelmed. But three months later, I was lucky if I got one message, text, or call a day. There had been so much outreach in the beginning, and then *nothing*. People who I thought would be there for me weren't, and those who I never thought would be were. Then there were those who either didn't say anything or said the wrong things. For example, one day during the first couple of months of Logan's treatment, I was sitting in the hallway at the hospital when a woman came up to me and we started chatting. Her son had been newly diagnosed, and I did my best to listen and offer words of encouragement until she said to me, "When we heard of our child's diagnosis, I thought, *At least it's not as bad as Logan's.*" *Um...excuse me?!* I let it go because I knew that she was still in the early stages of shock and disbelief over her child's diagnosis. But take note, people...this is something you should *never* say to another cancer parent—*period*! Cancer parents are supposed to support one another, not knock each other down. Then there were people whom I gave every opportunity to come to visit but never showed up, and there were those who would just show up at the worst times. No one could ever prepare for this situation, no matter what side of the coin you are on. And I totally get that everyone else had their own lives and their own things going on. But when I was trapped within those four walls for days on end with a sick child and only a quick treat of a Starbucks coffee once a day (if I was lucky to get out), it was really fucking hard! I had totally lost *all* patience for little things. I felt like I had become more of a bitch than I ever had been. I get that people didn't want to bother us at that point, but even a quick text or message to say, "Hey, I'm just thinking about you guys," or "You are in our prayers," would have meant so much. Saying and doing nothing made me feel worse. But with those quick messages, even if I couldn't always respond, they were just nice to see! I guess there is no right or wrong on either end of these circumstances. It is what it is.

This situation really made me appreciate what is important in life. I found joy in just going home to take a shower and get ready in my own bathroom. I enjoyed driving down the road with my sunroof open on a nice day. Hell, I would have even enjoyed walking barefoot in a thunderstorm at that point! I missed what every first-time mother experiences. It fucking sucked! I was angry, I was bitter, I was hurt, and I was upset.

But I was also exactly where I was meant to be. I love my son more than life itself, and I would do anything he needed to get better. I *hated* that he was going through this, but I was grateful that he would never remember it because he was still so young.

On Monday, July 10, right before Logan started round four of his aggressive inpatient chemotherapy treatment, he had a gastronomy tube (G-tube) placed. This is a tube that is inserted through the belly to bring nutrition directly to the stomach. Logan had stopped taking food by mouth after the second brain surgery and there hadn't been any progress in the right direction, so this was a decision we had to make. My husband and I were thinking this would be an easy surgery with a quick recovery. Boy, were we wrong! My poor baby had the worst and most difficult recovery based on where the G-tube was placed. He had overcome two major brain surgeries, so why would a simple stomach surgery be so bad?! It was bad because there was nothing but fat and tissue there, unlike in the brain, which doesn't feel pain. This poor kid was in so much pain. It was definitely the worst recovery yet, out of all the nine surgeries he had had up to that point. They had to (literally) blow up his stomach, put three buttons on the outside to hold it open, and then place what looked like the plug to a beach ball in his little belly. This poor kid!

They only gave him two days to recover before they started round four of chemo. They started his feeds at 2 milliliters per hour; that's next to nothing! There are 30 milliliters in an ounce, and babies at his age would normally drink about 2 ounces per hour, so that's about 1,440 milliliters per day. Dr. Weintraub said we could go home once Logan was tolerating 30 milliliters every hour. So, if we went at the rate of 1 milliliter per day, this would take too long, and he wouldn't be getting the necessary amount per day for proper nutrition. Once chemo started, Logan would tend to get sick more often, and understandably so. The doctors then started talking about possibly putting in a gastrostomy-jejunostomy tube (G-J tube) in a few weeks. This is a tube placed into the stomach and small intestine. That was when my mama-bear mode kicked in, and I said, "Absolutely *not*! He will learn to tolerate his feeds!" The problem was that when he would get sick, the nurses would typically turn off his feeds, which made no sense to me. They explained that they did this because they wanted to give his stomach time to settle, which I could understand. But how was his stomach supposed to learn how to push through? No pain, no gain...right?! So, I advocated for my son, and they stopped turning off his feeds. Sure enough, within twenty-one days, he went from 2 milliliters per hour to 30 milliliters per hour.

The part that sucked was that it was twenty-four hours a day. Another reason he was getting sick was that one of his antinausea meds was actually making him sick. (I was so thankful for one of our nurses who figured that out!) I knew my son would eventually be able to tolerate his feeds. He was strong, and he just needed to be given a chance! I couldn't wait until they switched him to bolus feeds, which would mean more volume and shorter times in between. He was taking milk by mouth via a syringe, and he loved it, but he was still struggling with the bottle. He loved playing with the nipple and getting milk as a surprise for doing so!

Logan recovered from round four of chemo better than all of the other rounds up to that point, and we were able to go home sooner than anyone had expected. *Rock star status!* But I had a traumatic realization during this time regarding Logan's diagnosis and progress. We were talking with one of Logan's neurosurgery residents—whom we loved—and as we were discussing his diagnosis and the brain surgeries, out of nowhere I blurted out, "*What?!* They removed a part of his brain?! How did I not know this?! Why didn't anyone tell me?!" My husband told me I knew. The doctors told me I knew. Hell, I had seen the damn images! So why didn't I know in that moment? I think I had compartmentalized it until I was ready to deal with it, which makes total sense. I had had so much thrown at me on a daily basis, and this had been a *huge* thing to deal with. No wonder why the doctors had kept telling me he may have deficiencies. *Duh!* Actually, realizing this and accepting the fact that they had removed a part of my son's left frontal lobe was so devastating for me to deal with. I think I cried for two days straight. That's why Dr. Adamo had gone in to do the tumor resection twice, and so quickly, because baby's brains are so soft and have the plasticity to recover from trauma. Plus, because Logan hadn't yet learned certain things from that part of his brain, the other parts of his brain could then compensate. Basically, he would just learn to do things from different parts of his brain. And because we were lucky enough to have the best doctors in Albany, and because Dr. Lucas was closely monitoring Logan's progress, I had no doubt that he would recover from any deficiencies he may come up against. So, we just pushed through chemo and continued with his physical therapy, occupational therapy, and speech therapy. Once we could be home on a more permanent basis, we would also have early intervention services to assist with Logan's ongoing treatment. We still had a very long road ahead of us, but I knew my kid was such a fighter, and I felt so proud to be his mom!

CHAPTER
9

BEFORE WE WERE able to go home for thirteen days after Logan's fourth round of chemo, we received "good news" at this time when, after the second brain surgery, Dr. Adamo and Dr. Weintraub learned that Logan's brain tumor was actually graded a two, three, and four, making it rarer and more treatable than initially thought. They were more hopeful about Logan's treatment plan, his survival and longevity, and the probability that the tumor would not come back.

Thirteen days was the longest period we had been able to go home up to this point. Logan's counts had recovered more quickly than they had expected after round four, and as much as I wanted to go home, the thought of being away from the hospital still gave me anxiety. Being home meant that we would have to do everything ourselves. I couldn't just push a call button for a nurse or a PCA to come help if Logan got sick, or if I needed to shower or run out for a cup of coffee. (I blame Albany Medical Center for my Starbucks addiction; it was my ten minutes of "me time" every day, getting out of the hospital and walking across the street for my triple grande skinny vanilla latte fix.) I couldn't help but wonder what we were going to do once round five was done—then we would *really* be on our own!

On the eve of Logan's fifth round of inpatient chemo (which was also my birthday), I was so overcome with con-flicting emotions. Part of me was excited to go back to the hospital and finish inpatient chemo once and for all. But there was another part of me that just wanted to stop and not do any more chemo. I was emotionally, mentally, and physically exhausted. While I would have never *not* done that final round of chemo, the thought did cross my mind. Just knowing the discomfort Logan was in was killing me.

He had made so much progress at home! He was doing well with transitions, like moving from sitting to lying down. He liked to be held, and he didn't fuss as much for diaper changes. He was actively trying with the binky and the bottle. He was swallowing very well. He was putting his hands in his mouth, and we even found a tickle spot—and boy, who doesn't like baby giggles?! He became very observant and interactive, making all sorts of noises and entertaining himself. He was doing *normal* baby stuff! It was such a wonderful thing to see!

My biggest fear with going back in for one more round of inpatient chemo was that we would lose this great progress he had made in the less than two weeks we'd had him at home. *What if he regressed?* My guilt became overwhelming. *Did my baby know that in a matter of days after starting round five he was going to feel like shit again and would not want to move or be touched? Did he know that he was once again going to be throwing up all the time and would be forced to do therapies while his body was in excruciating pain?* It fucking sucked. He couldn't tell us what was wrong, what he was feeling, or what he wanted to do. We were always guessing and trusting our instincts. It was—and still is—so hard! My only positive thought at that time was that this would be his *last* round of inpatient chemo!

While, yes, the chemo was working for the massive tumor

that was in Logan's head, we were now also faced with the seriousness of him having a brain injury. The part of Logan's brain that had been removed was the part that primarily controlled his language and impulse control. It had been hard enough dealing with our three-and-a-half-month-old child having a deadly brain tumor and hearing that there was nothing they could do and that he wouldn't survive. Then, after they had been cautiously optimistic, we had to put all our strength and faith in trusting that the doctors would do the right thing. And then there was the thought of what chemo was doing to Logan's body—he could lose his hearing and/or his eyesight, he may never be able to have kids, he was vomiting all the time, and we had to wear gloves to change his diaper because of the toxicity of the chemo. Now, on top of all of that, they were telling us that he may never walk, or he may be paralyzed or have a stroke, not just from the surgeries but from all the trauma that had been done to his body and his brain. *How the hell did this all happen?* As we were still fighting to save Logan's life from the congenital glioblastoma, we were adding a traumatic brain injury to the mix. *Oh, my fucking God...why, just why?!* It never got any easier. Some days I was angry, and some days I was full of faith. And while every day I knew Logan had chosen us to be his parents for a reason, it still *fucking sucked*!

What frustrated me then (and still does, to this day) was when people would express to me how happy they were about Logan's progress. I didn't always respond as positively as most would think. People would say, "Aren't you happy/excited/ecstatic?" And to be honest, not really! Yes, I was glad to hear that most of the tumor had now been removed, but that was minor compared to the big picture of the situation we would be dealing with for years to come. Our son was diagnosed with a congenital glioblastoma. He was born with cancer. But this would be just a small battle won in the long war we would have to fight! While we (my husband and I, and our families) appreciated the thoughts and positive comments, Logan was *not* in the clear—and he wouldn't be...*ever*! He was born with a brain tumor and would always be at risk of it returning one day. Even though we were preparing for his final round of inpatient chemo, this fight was far from over!

Logan's last round of aggressive inpatient chemo lasted for about three weeks. Living in the hospital again was the worst. I was always having to pack a bag to stay with my baby for weeks on end, and that is *not* the way any new mom expects to live her life! (Thankfully, I was able to come home every few days, even if it was just for a shower or to get a good night's sleep.) I literally had to pack a suitcase for each hospital stay. By that point, I could probably write a book on how to prepare for a weeklong stay at the hospital. We had it down to a science. We would use storage bins for Logan's toys and wipes (I hated the wipes the hospital supplied), plus butt wipes for me because the hospital toilet paper was paper-thin (it was always getting stuck...*gross*). Then there was a suitcase for my clothes and another suitcase for Logan's clothes, plus grocery bags for snacks and bottles of water. Oh, and I always brought my breast pump and supplies since I was still pumping through this. The doctors were actually surprised I was still producing milk as mental and emotional trauma can affect production. I knew the importance of breast milk for my baby's health, and I vowed that I would get him through chemo with breast milk. Plus, I had overproduced before he had been diagnosed, so I was always ahead of the game. Thankfully, the hospital provided diapers, and Logan was still fed via a pump, so I didn't have to worry about his changing supplies or food. I would joke and say that the three best things to come from hospital life and Logan being diagnosed as a baby were: (1) free diapers while we lived in the hospital, (2) because he was so young, he probably won't remember any of it, and (3) he got his drug habit out of the way early. (Get it? Chemo, ha ha... I know, funny-not-funny, but you have to find some humor in this journey.)

We finished round five on September 20, 2017. After that, the outpatient chemo was planned to start after his counts had recovered. This would be another eight rounds of outpatient treatment, at forty to fifty days each, so his immune system would pretty much be compromised for the next fourteen months or so. This also meant that we couldn't send Logan to day care. I had recently made the decision to take a leave of absence from work until the end of the year because I had been trying too hard to juggle everything, and Logan—obviously—came first. This was hard because at Aflac more than 50 percent of my business is done in the fourth quarter for a January 1 start date, so I was not only missing out on seeing my clients, but that time of year was also when I could really thrive financially. But it wouldn't have been fair to my clients to only be available part-time. And it wouldn't have been fair to my son—he came first; always has, always will. I had to (and I did) trust those who were helping me in my business to do right by my clients. That's why I was working with a team, and why it was so important for me to be choosy about who I worked with (and I still am). With Logan being immunocompromised, we couldn't send him to day care, and we couldn't just have random babysitters or friends and family watch him. And now with the outpatient chemo starting, my schedule was about to get really crazy. We had to be very careful! This was our baby's life that was at risk here!

One positive thing that happened during this time was that Logan had been approved for early intervention through the county. They had squeezed in his evaluation before we had gone back to the hospital for round five. We were excited to learn that all of his therapies could be done at home, and we wouldn't have to travel or take him anywhere. He qualified for physical therapy (PT), occupational therapy (OT), speech/feeding therapy, and special education. I was always doing some type of exercise, stretching, or activity with him, but having professional help and guidance was going to be awesome!

While we were always positive that Logan would beat cancer (or should I say, "smack the puck out of cancer,"), we weren't prepared for what life was going to be like outside of the hospital, or what his future needs would be. We had lived at Albany Med for the better part of six months. *Holy shit! How was that even possible?!* In the beginning, when he was first diagnosed, I couldn't wait to be on the other side of this. And here we were, making progress toward that goal. While those six months flew by, they also were the longest six months ever. My baby hadn't even turned one yet and he had already gone through a horrible cancer diagnosis (and prognosis), several rounds of aggressive chemotherapy, two major brain surgeries, several blood transfusions, vomiting every day, getting a G-tube for nutrition, not to mention countless therapies—and that was just what *he* went through. Kevin and I had also fought our own personal battles. Our marriage had struggled, and we were working hard to save it while we were trying to save our kid's life. I had to give up my job, and while that was only temporary, I am a natural-born worker—it's in my blood. I couldn't volunteer or do any of my beloved extracurricular activities such as teaching or taking dance classes, going to the gym, or anything else. I had to keep myself just as safe as Logan. I was *not* going to risk him getting sick or getting an infection because of me. It was bad enough that we had to put his vaccines on hold, I wasn't going to be that mom who would put my son at risk in unnecessary situations! This was about Logan—his survival, his life, and his legacy. Yet, despite it all, I would always come back to knowing that Logan had chosen me to be his mom for a reason, because he trusted I would get him through this.

CHAPTER
10

AFTER LOGAN'S FIFTH round of inpatient chemo, now the real work was to begin! No more pushing the nurses' call button when Logan would get sick or had a blowout (you know, when your baby poops and it is literally *all over*, up his back and front), or when I needed a break. No more doctors, nurses, or PAs waking us up in the middle of the night to check Logan's vitals. No more help with feeds or therapies.

What?! You mean I have to do this on my own now? I didn't sign up for this. Oh, wait, yes I did—that's what it means to be a mom. But no, not like this. There had been no normalcy for us, never had been and never would be. But how could I do this alone?!

As much as I wanted to feel excited about being done with inpatient chemo, I had no clue how the hell I was supposed to do *all* of it by myself. Yes, my husband helped when he wasn't working, my in-laws were with us when they were in town, and my mother helped when she was available, but the day-to-day stuff was all about to be on me. Logan was technically cancer-free at this point, but that is such a subjective term. There was no evidence of disease (NED), but he still had to go through treatment. Now we had eight rounds of outpatient chemo that would happen over the next year, at least. *How was I going to do this?!*

This was when it became an extremely lonely experience for me. Kevin was back to work full-time, and I felt guilty asking my mother-in-law for help all the time when they were in town. Both of my parents worked full-time. Our friends all had full-time jobs and families of their own. So, it was always just me during the day—alone—to not only take care of a sick baby but to also maintain a household and get some of my own work done, not to mention trying to work out and do "me" stuff.

How hard is it to take care of a sick baby? Well... I would get up at five in the morning, get Logan's meds ready, work out (if I was lucky), and get his feed up by six. (This meant carefully measuring his formula and water, pouring it into a feeding pack, then carefully placing the tube through the feeding pump and hooking it into Logan's stomach.) Then I would shower and get ready before my husband got up to go to work, otherwise, a shower just wouldn't happen if I waited until later in the day. From there, my day would become a blur. Logan would wake up around seven. He was a pretty good sleeper and slept through the night most days. He would need four medicines by nine in the morning! We then would do some physical therapy and stretches, and we'd practice sitting up. We would also practice using the bottle. By the time we were done with that, it was usually time for his morning nap (if he felt like taking one that day). I then had at least one load of laundry to do from the morning or the day before. I would try to update his followers on Facebook because at the time he was still in treatment, and I would post updates (or at least try to) daily. After posting an update on Logan's progress, I would check both my personal and business emails. Once that was done, it would be time for more therapy where I would try to sit him up and try the bottle again. At ten months old, Logan still wasn't strong enough to sit up on his own. He looked like a bobblehead because the poor kid had been lying in a hospital bed, flat on his back, for over seven months! The back of his head was flat. It was sad to see. Babies are born with two major soft spots on the top of the head; these are called fontanels. These soft spots are spaces between the bones of the skull, which allow the skull to be molded during birth, and it can take up to eighteen months after birth for the bones to fully form. Our home care nurse had once mentioned getting a helmet for Logan, and I had no clue what she was talking about. She had explained that a helmet would help mold Logan's skull into shape, and they were more commonly used than one would think. Why hadn't the doctors, nurses, or therapists ever mentioned this to me? Probably simply because there had always been so much in our journey that was just trial and error and learning on our own or by osmosis! Seriously, there is no fucking handbook for this shit! So, in December 2017, we proved medical necessity and got insurance approval, and Logan was fitted for his helmet, which he wore for about ten months—and you bet your ass we decorated that shit! We found a local artist (actually, an art teacher at a local school), who painted his helmet blue with "Puck Cancer" on the back, along with the Union logo (we are huge Union hockey fans) and the New York Rangers logo, and on the front, it said "Logan Strong™," with a small cartoonish photo of Wolverine. Later, when Logan was just about done with treatment in September 2018 (you will read more about that in Chapter 13), we changed his helmet to black and gray and put "Logan smacked the puck out of cancer," on the back with the dates of his treatment, but I won't reveal those dates here—you'll just have to keep reading! Anyway, back to my day-to-day routine... On days when we didn't have a doctor's appointment or any other places to be, I would make phone calls for Logan's care and treatment. Whether it was scheduling a doctor's appointment, arranging his home visits or early intervention, or dealing with insurance, there was always something. I was always overwhelmed, and I always had a million things going on in my head. People would often ask me, "Aren't you happy to be home?" Yes, I was, but it was *so much harder* at home. I was "on" all day long, and the next thing I knew, my husband would be home from work and it would be time to make dinner. Then Logan's feed would go up one last time and we would do his nightly meds, along with having to flush his PICC lines. (A PICC line, or peripherally inserted central catheter, is a thin, soft, long tube that is inserted into a vein, in this case, in Logan's chest. This catheter is positioned in a large vein that carries blood into the heart and is used for long-term intravenous or

IV antibiotics, nutrition, or medications such as chemo, and for blood draws.)

In looking back on all of this, I need to remind myself (because I'm human, and my memory sucks—moms get chemo brain too!) that Logan truly is a miracle. They said he wouldn't survive, and yet the irony is that I am here today, writing this chapter on Veteran's Day, which is when this journey began exactly five years ago. So, even though it's not easy to relive everything we've gone through, I will never take for granted that miracles really do happen, and Logan has proven that over and over again.

We finished Logan's first round of outpatient chemo, but not without a terrible hiccup along the way. Now, what I am about to share is not meant to get anyone in trouble. The situation was handled, and we were satisfied with how everything had turned out. I'm sharing it here because it was a part of our journey. It happened, it was stressful, and it was just one more fucking thing we had to handle. Shit happens, life happens, and people make mistakes. To this day, whenever I hear someone say they had a bad experience at Albany Med, I find myself sticking up for the hospital. I don't think people truly understand that a hospital is a business, and doctors and nurses are people too. So, when I share this hiccup, don't be mad or upset for us—it's OK! Really! This was a pure case of human error, and while that human error could have been severe, it wasn't, and we are grateful. We chose to handle it gracefully and directly, and we are content with how it turned out.

On one of the days when we had gone in for Logan's outpatient chemo, my mother-in-law was with me. We typically would schedule Logan's appointments for the mornings to try to work around his feeding schedule, although that didn't always work out. But we liked morning appointments because they let us rest for the remainder of the day. Well, not on this day! We were in a patient room in the Melodies Center, and as the nurse was hooking up Logan's chemo, the pump that administered the treatment kept getting an error. OK, no big deal. Maybe the battery was dead or dying, or maybe the pump needed to be reset. So, the nurse went and got another pump, but the same thing happened. She kept getting an error. She tried a third pump, and the same thing happened. After the second pump had shown an error, I already knew something was off. I had been doing this long enough at that point to know. The nurse had seen my concern and frustration, and as she was playing with the third pump, she suggested that my mother-in-law and I go to lunch. Now, you may be thinking, *Oh my god, she is leaving her baby in that situation?!* I was completely comfortable doing so because, as I mentioned, we'd been going through treatment long enough at that point that I knew he was in good hands. So, we went across the street to Panera and enjoyed a somewhat relaxing lunch.

When we got back to the room, Dr. Weintraub was in there waiting for us. She had a look of anguish and she asked me to sit down.

I said, "What's going on?"

She cut to the chase and said, "We fucked up. And by 'we,' I mean the pharmacy."

Immediately I was on high alert, and I asked, "Okay, what happened?"

She explained that Logan's chemotherapy had been drawn as an adult dose, which was why the pump had been getting an error message—the consistency was too thick to run through that particular tube and pump. My first concern was obviously, *What did or does this do to Logan? Is he OK?!* She assured me that if something had happened it would have happened while the chemo was being administered, and since he had only received half the dose, he was OK. *Would there be any effects later that day or beyond?* Again, she reassured me that he was fine and said we should just keep an extra eye on him that night. This was outpatient chemo, and of course, we would have wanted to go home, but my mama-bear instinct kicked in and I said, "Nope, we aren't taking him home. You fucked up, so you watch him!" She agreed and got us an inpatient bed for the night.

Thankfully, Dr. Weintraub and I had developed a special bond through this whole process. Even now, almost five years later, every time I see her, she says to me, "Remember when I told you he wouldn't survive, or he would never walk?" She follows that with, "What the hell do I know?!" It's great how she *loves* that she had been wrong, and she really treats Logan like he is one of her own.

Later on that day, the head of the pharmacy came up (he had just started there very recently) and apologized to us for the mistake. Yes, I was angry, and I wanted to know how the hell this could have happened, but I knew anger wasn't going to do anyone any good. I accepted his apology and asked him to relay a message to the person who had been responsible for Logan's chemotherapy orders and please tell them I forgave them. You see, I was worried about how that person was feeling. To this day, I don't know who it was; I just knew that if I had done that, I would have felt badly enough without having a worried parent yelling at me. I didn't want to escalate the situation with my anger or relay it to that person only to have them commit suicide over this—yes, I literally thought about that. This was a *huge* mistake that could have gone worse, but we were blessed and grateful that it hadn't. Due to this, the pharmacy at Albany Med put new protocols in place to add an extra label to their orders that says "pediatric," or something to that effect. It's an extra step of checks and balances when administering drugs, and it wouldn't have been thought of unless something like this had happened.

The next morning, Dr. Weintraub came up to check on us and said, "I have to tell you something."

I thought to myself, *What now?*

With hesitation, she said, "It's been decided that we won't charge you for this hospital stay."

I looked at her and laughed. She kinda laughed too. (She's a mom, and she knew what the potential severity could have been.) I said, "You didn't overcook my steak!" She agreed and understood exactly what I meant.

So, as Logan's first round of outpatient chemo was wrapping up, even with that hiccup, I was trying to work more because the fourth quarter is the busiest time in my business. On some days, I would get up early and go to work, leave to bring Logan for his treatment, and then go back to work. Our nanny and mother-in-law were so helpful during those times. That was my life, and that *is still* my life. But I did—and will continue to do—*whatever* it takes to not only help my son but to also keep my sanity! I have my moments and my hard days but looking at my precious little boy's face always gives me the strength to keep going. I must say to myself, at least once a day, how gorgeous my kid is!

During this time, I finally decided to see a counselor, but I was concerned about whether I would be able to bond with them. I was given two recommendations for counselors who specialized in what we were going through. One was about fifteen minutes from us, and the other was about an hour away. Naturally, I called the one closest to us first. The first thing this person said to me was, "What insurance do you have?" *Um, really? My child is fighting for his life battling cancer and you want to ask me what fucking insurance I have? No, thank you!* So I called the one who was an hour away, and they didn't even ask about my insurance, they just scheduled the appointment and said to bring my insurance information with me and they would figure it out. We have been seeing that counselor, Gerry, ever since. Sometimes I would go alone, sometimes my husband would go alone, and sometimes we would go together. Thankfully, we can even do virtual visits now, which makes it so much easier to schedule. Even when that wasn't the case, we had found someone we resonated with, so it was worth the drive!

I was feeling frustrated at the time because no matter who I talked to (professional or not), they would always say something like, "You have every right to feel the way you do." *No fucking shit...thanks for the permission!* While this was true, I just wished I didn't feel some of the ways I did a lot of the time. Little things would piss me off, and I always wondered why. But I've since come to learn that little shit bothered me—and still does—because I know the travesty of the big shit. The little shit makes me bitchy because it doesn't—and shouldn't—matter. It's all about perspective. Early on in Logan's treatment, I explained to Courtney, (the social worker at the Melodies Center) that I was so bitchy and that little shit kept getting under my skin. She told me that that was normal, and it was OK for me to be a crappy person sometimes. I said, jokingly, "Can I get that as a card or something, please?" And she delivered! On the back of her business card, she wrote: "This card grants you permission to be a *crappy human.* You are doing enough. Let the rest go." I laminated that card, and I still carry it with me to this day.

There are still times when I am miserable or I cry for seemingly no reason, or I am mean, just because. No one should have to live this life, but *this is my life.*

One of the things I appreciated most from Gerry was that he said I needed to reach out to people more, instead of waiting for them to reach out to me. He told me that because most people don't want to intrude or don't know how to act or what to say, I would need to be the one to initiate the conversation. This was an eye-opener for me because I had been feeling and thinking the opposite; I thought that people needed to reach out to me. But the truth was, the adrenaline was now gone, the mama fight mode had faded, and the reality of our lives had settled in. Gerry also told me that I had every right to grieve or to not want to do certain things with friends who have "normal" children and that it was normal for me to feel that way. That made me feel good. Jealousy of people who have "normal" kids is *real* and it *hurts.* This is still hard for me because I want to do those things, but not only am I super overprotective of Logan and his immune system, but I also find myself comparing Logan's progress to my friends' kids who are the same age or even younger. It's so much easier said than done not to do that! I'm a constant work in progress.

And in the meantime, Logan was continuing to kick cancer's ass. We ended up starting his second round of outpatient chemo a week early because my kid is a freaking rock star and his counts recovered quicker than they thought they would. He was also holding his head up on his own, and we began planning his first birthday party!

CHAPTER
11

WHEN "THEY" TELL you your child won't survive, that he won't ever walk or talk, and "they" all turn out to be wrong, you celebrate like there's no tomorrow when your child turns a year old. And that is *exactly* what we did. We went *all out* for Logan's first birthday celebration, which we were able to hold on his actual birthday because it fell on a Saturday, November 18, 2017.

By that time, Logan was on his second round of outpatient chemo, and Dr. Weintraub even let us plan his treatment around his birthday party. Yes, that's right, we planned our son's cancer treatment around his first birthday party.

We were so grateful that Dr. Weintraub understood how significant this day was, and that she respected that, as a family and as new parents, we needed this celebration more than anything.

Can you guess what we chose as the theme for his first birthday party?! *Superheroes!* Yep, we had a #tinysuperhero celebration, and of course, we asked everyone to dress up as their favorite superhero! We learned quickly that whatever we were planning for Logan's birthday party theme would also have to match his Halloween costume, which he would be wearing just a few weeks before his birthday. It was a win-win! A friend of mine made his Wolverine costume for us. She even came over a couple of times to measure Logan and to make sure the costume would fit over his MIC-KEY button (another name for a G-tube) and his port access. Why was he Wolverine, you ask? Well, Wolverine's real name is Logan, and during Logan's treatment we had received a personalized autographed photo of Hugh Jackman (who plays Wolverine), addressed to Logan. It said, "To the real superhero, keep fighting, Bub." *Cool, right?!* At first, we had no clue where the autograph had come from. I even Googled the return address but couldn't come up with any answers. I also looked up Hugh Jackman's signature to compare it to the one on Logan's autograph, and it turned out to be the real deal. After my "expert" detective work, there was only one person I thought it could have come from. I had an old friend from middle school, who I knew worked in the movie industry. I reached out and asked if it was from him, and he said yes. Here was someone whom I hadn't seen in over thirty years, and he had done something purely out of the kindness of his heart, without looking for any recognition. *How sweet is that?!* Later on, this same friend also got us some original signed posters from Stan Lee, which we used in our first fundraiser. We also gifted one to Dr. Adamo because he is a huge comic book fan. (When we first received the posters, I had asked my husband who "Stanley" was. He just laughed and corrected me. I was either *that oblivious*, or my mama cancer brain had been in full effect.)

Logan's first birthday party celebration was *amazing*! We had rented the banquet hall at our church's parish center, and our family and close friends all worked tirelessly that morning to decorate and set everything up. The party was catered by our favorite local restaurant, the Mohawk Taproom and Grill, and our favorite local bakery, Villa Italia, made an awesome superhero sheet cake with less than twenty-four hours' notice. (I had originally ordered a three-tiered cake from another bakery, but it had looked nothing like what I had ordered and was delivered with animals in the car—*gross!*) A friend of mine made some yummy sweet treats as well! Throughout the week leading up to the party, Kevin had made some very fun and creative superhero games. We also had goodie bags and a photo booth, and my friend made really cool giant letter blocks that spelled "LOGAN"; they were about two feet square. We still have them, and we use them every year for Logan's birthday and the Logan Strong™ Foundation golf tournaments.

We invited all our closest friends, our favorite nurses, our work colleagues, and of course, our families. I also invited my three closest cancer mamas whom I had met on this journey. (I will share more about them later.) There was hand sanitizer—or as we called it, "superhero sanitizer"—at every table. Also, on the invitations, we had asked everyone to have their flu shot, and if they were feeling ill that day, to not attend, as Logan's health was (and still is) our priority. We had the corner area of the banquet hall set up for Logan, and we only allowed a few people to hold him to keep him as safe and protected as possible.

As much as this wasn't how I had envisioned my baby's first birthday party, after everything we had been through up to that point, it was a much-deserved celebration. We were celebrating Logan's first birthday after the doctors had told us several times that he wouldn't survive. This was just one of many milestones to come! In lieu of gifts, we asked everyone to write a letter to Logan for him to read on his eighteenth birthday and/or to make a donation in Logan's name to the Melodies Center for Childhood Cancer and Blood Disorders at Albany Medical Center. We knew that Logan had such a journey ahead of him and would have such a story to tell. And what better way to commemorate all of his accomplishments than with letters from those who were there in the beginning of his journey? I had heard of this idea on social media or in a news story, and I thought it would be perfect for Logan. Not many people remember much from childhood, and even less from their first years. I wanted to be able to share these special memories and the truth of Logan's story with him later in life. Our friends and family could write him a letter, whatever they wanted it to include, and we would then open and share them with him on his eighteenth birthday. (I can't wait to read all those letters then!)

After celebrating Logan's birthday, we were able to spend Thanksgiving, Christmas, and New Year's together at home. As exciting as that was, this was the start of my ongoing struggle with the holidays. Yes, we were able to celebrate all his firsts with these holidays the year before, before he had been diagnosed. But we had missed (and still miss) the normalcy of a child's excitement for the holidays. Logan didn't know any different; he didn't know when it was his birthday, he didn't know when it was Thanksgiving or Christmas. These things don't resonate with him due to his brain injury, which is why holidays are always so tough for me, whether it's a long three-day weekend for Memorial Day or a major holiday like Christmas or Easter. It sucks! The "good" part of this is that we don't have to go overboard with gifts, but we still like to get him at least one significant gift for his birthday and Christmas. So we save time and money in that regard (heck, he still has brand-new toys in his closet that I could wrap), but that's not the point; the point is that my child doesn't understand holidays, and it fucking sucks.

There is so much of our journey that has sucked—and still does—but I do my best to stay positive, to keep moving forward, and do my best for my son and my husband. I have to remind myself every day that this is *our journey*, and we were chosen for a reason. To be brutally honest, not everyone could fucking handle something like this—and I don't say that to be an asshole, I say that because I've lived it and

I know it's the truth! But the funny thing is, I had never thought I could be the kind of person who could handle this, and I ended up surprising myself!

As I've been writing this book, I have been looking back at some of the blog posts I had written during this journey. And in reflecting on the first year of Logan's life and our cancer journey, I found it fitting to share my blog post from December 31, 2017, verbatim:

2017 Reflection

As I look back on this past year, I am filled with mixed emotions. It has been by far the worst year of my life, but also the best year of my life. I have learned so much, especially in these past ten months. I am not the same person I was this time last year. I am changed, I am better, and I am stronger! I have transformed both personally and professionally, as a mother, a wife, a daughter, and a friend. I have gained many new, valued friendships, and I have let go of some that weren't so healthy. I have more patience and kindness. I have found inner strength and courage I didn't know I had. I have added way more to my plate than I could have ever imagined possible, but it has taught me how to balance. (I would have never thought this situation would teach me about balance.) I am more focused in how I spend my time and with whom I spend my time. So much good has come out of this bad situation.

So, to sum it up, I've learned:

...to have more patience and kindness

...to trust and believe in my faith

...to believe in God's greater plan

...to ask for help when I need it

...to balance my time

...to juggle a million things at once

...to put my son and my family first

...to focus on the positive

...that I am stronger than I ever imagined I could be

...that I have some really great friends

...that I also have (or had*) some really shitty friends*

...what is important

...when to let go and when to walk away

...way too many names of medicines and procedures I never thought I would know

...that most people are good

...that people don't always know what to say, or don't always say the right thing

...that at the end of the day family is all that matters

...that everything happens for a reason

...to live every day to the fullest

...to let myself feel any emotion

...that my son is truly a miracle

...that my husband actually has emotions

...that I am truly blessed with the best in-laws and parents

...that childhood cancer awareness needs more funding

...that I work for an amazing *company*

...how thankful I am to the people near and far who have reached out, even if just to share an encouraging word. They say it takes a village, and we are so truly grateful for the village that has encompassed us all in love.

And the biggest *things I have learned are that faith* always *wins and miracles* do *happen!*

Thank you all for being on this journey with us! Wishing you all a safe, happy, and healthy 2018! We are all #LoganStrong.

—*#MamaStrong*

In January 2018, Children's Healthcare of Atlanta (CHOA) chose Logan's story to share with the entire Aflac sales force at their kick-off meetings across the country. That's over 16,000 independent benefits consultants in the US with over 500,000 accounts and close to ten million policyholders! Logan's story would be shared to help raise awareness about childhood cancer and future funding opportunities for Aflac's Cancer and Blood Disorders Center of CHOA. These children who are battling cancer are innocent, and yet they're suffering and fighting every day—and, in a lot of cases, they need nothing short of a miracle. We hoped that by sharing about our journey we could do our part to support the cause.

CHOA flew their film crew and marketing team up from

Atlanta, and they basically turned our house into a film studio. It was very overwhelming and exhilarating at the same time! They made Kevin and I feel very comfortable, and they helped us tell Logan's story clearly and concisely. The crew was also able to interview Logan's doctors (Dr. Weintraub and Dr. Adamo) at Albany Med. Together, we were able to share our journey of what Logan had been through and how CHOA's treatment plan helped save our baby's life. The film crew and the marketing team were extremely friendly and were in such awe of Logan and his accomplishments to that point. The whole situation was very surreal for everyone involved. No one would have ever thought that something like this would literally come full circle. I think the film crew and marketing team were just as excited to be a part of this experience as we were to share it. And Logan? Well, he just loved the attention and all the bright lights!

Today, I am a co-ambassador for CHOA, along with Jackie Williams, a colleague at Aflac. I still donate monthly, and I increase my donation every year. I have yet to visit the hospital and meet the doctors who wrote the treatment plan that saved my son's life, but that is definitely a bucket list item! (To learn more about Children's Healthcare of Atlanta and how you can help, please visit the "How to Help" section at the end of this book.)

A few months later, we reached Logan's one-year cancer diagnosis anniversary—March 8, 2018—the day my life had changed forever. When I became a mom for the first time at the age of forty, I never thought that becoming a cancer mom would be part of the package. When we first heard Logan's diagnosis, I thought my life was over. My world had been shattered and my heart was broken into a million pieces. I had already been through a lot in my life—being beaten up by an ex-boyfriend, having thousands of dollars and a vehicle stolen from me, among other disastrous things—but nothing could have prepared me to hear the words, "Your child has cancer." No one should *ever* have to hear the word "cancer," especially when it's about your child—a baby, nonetheless.

As I reflected on that first year and everything that had happened, it all seemed so crazy. The emotions and experiences we had been through were so unreal. Thinking about it all was like watching a movie of my life. (I half-jokingly say that our life would make a great reality show if it wasn't for HIPAA!) This wasn't supposed to have happened; this couldn't have been real...but it was! And as much as Logan's first year was painful, it also showed me that everything happens for a reason and that our son had chosen us to be his parents. There had been way too many coincidences that had happened over that first year to make me believe otherwise. Too many people had come into our lives for a reason and at just the right time. It was all so surreal!

I now know firsthand that we aren't promised tomorrow. But you can bet your ass that I am going to enjoy every moment with my son, and I will keep fighting until the day I die for him to survive and get the best damn care there is! I hate the "C word," and I hate that I am a cancer mom, but I *love* my son. I did—and will still do—anything for him to make him better and provide him with the best opportunities in life. I didn't wish for my son to grow up fast (no parent does), but I remember wishing for those times to become a distant memory. So, as much as I still hate that I am a cancer mom, I am also *proud* to be a cancer mom, and I am even more proud to be Logan's mom! I have always been open in sharing about Logan's treatment, progress, delays, and milestones—all the positive and negative happenings. I didn't sugarcoat anything about that first year. I am real, I am raw, and I am unapologetically me. It wasn't easy *at all*, but we did it—and we keep on doing it every day!

It was honestly a celebration that we had made it to Logan's one-year diagnosis anniversary. It meant that he had survived, and he had proven all the doctors and experts wrong! I always knew that Logan would beat cancer, but what I hadn't expected—and what no one had prepared me for—were the developmental delays that would lie ahead. *What were they? Would they be only temporary? Were they from the cancer, from the chemo, or from the brain injury?* The unanswered questions were constantly on my mind. (And they still are!) Just because Logan was almost done with chemo, that didn't mean we didn't still have a long road of healing ahead of us. Logan had had a piece of his brain removed where the tumor had been. Thankfully, because of his age, he had the opportunity to overcome any delays or deficiencies. But we still had a lot of work to do. He was getting physical therapy and occupational therapy twice a week each. He was also receiving special education and music therapy once a week. We were so grateful for all the services that were available to us, but it was a constant struggle trying to figure things out. It was so hard because Logan couldn't tell us what was wrong, and trying to figure out if he was tired, hungry, or constipated was a constant struggle. Was he hitting his head because he had a headache, or did his ears hurt, or was it from the brain injury? There was so much that we were still trying to figure out with his development, both with his physical body and his brain. The developmental delays were what bothered me the most. It was like I was mourning the loss of having a "normal" child—the baby that all parents envision, who walks, talks, crawls, and eats—that is what I thought of as "normal," and we didn't have that. Logan hadn't taken a bottle since he was five months old. At sixteen months old, he could barely stand, even though he should have been walking by then. He had never crawled, nor had more than five minutes of tummy time. That hurt!

When people would say to me, "I don't know how you do it, you're so strong," I used to respond by saying, "You would do it too if it were your kid." But the truth is, I don't know if everyone would or could. I think the fact that we had waited until we were in our forties and were established in our careers really helped with our understanding and with dealing with Logan's diagnosis, which in turn helped with his progress. He was doing as well as he was because of who my husband and I are; the doctors had even said that. They still say that we are the reason he has survived and thrived. The medical world had failed him, but we all proved them wrong. And I don't say this to "toot our own horns"; I say this because we are positive people by nature, and we truly try to see the good in any situation. We both have done so much good in our lives and have given back by donating our time and money to help others. That is why Logan continues to do so well, and it's why we have such a strong support system...because we worked our asses off for it, and dammit, we deserve it! We have always had the right people come into our lives at the right times throughout this whole journey. Why? Because we deserve it, because Logan deserves it, and because it is God's plan! Logan is here for a reason, and we are *not* giving up—*ever*!

Yes, our situation has sucked, but sitting around and crying about it wouldn't have made it any better. Did I allow myself moments? Abso-fucking-lutely! I've had plenty of moments, but I don't let myself stay there for long because what is that going to solve? Where is that going to get me or my son? My son is a fighter because his father and I are fighters. I was now back to work full-time, I became the president of the Logan Strong Foundation, and I was a Rotarian, a mom, and a wife. It was exhausting. But it also drove me! I now had a mission in life to help raise awareness about childhood cancer and help to provide support to others who were fighting this terrible disease!

So, in honor of all that we had been through in that first year, I wanted to do something positive to remember that day. I decided that I wanted to *celebrate* Logan's annual cancerversary, rather than mourning that day. The fact that we had made it to one year was *huge*, especially considering that we had been told numerous times that our son wasn't going to survive, and he continued—and still continues—to overcome and prove that he truly is our miracle baby! We wanted to celebrate every day, not to mention a *year* of fighting and beating cancer!

CHAPTER
12

BY THIS POINT in our story, you've started to see some of the "coincidences" that came our way and how we had escaped the worst-case scenarios throughout our journey. And while I am still more spiritual than I am religious, I know where and when to give credit when credit is due, and in this case, the credit goes to God.

Let me start with how I was raised. My father was (and still is) an atheist, and my mother had been raised Catholic. My father hadn't wanted to baptize me, but my maternal grandfather had refused to have a grandchild who was not baptized, and since my father had been baptized Lutheran, they had agreed that I would be baptized as well. My mother and my father did not raise me in the church; they wanted me to find my own way and make my own decisions. Before meeting my husband in 2011, I had only been to church maybe a dozen times. I would go for Christmas or New Year's Eve, and on special occasions like baptisms, weddings, and funerals. I had never disbelieved in God, but I never *really* believed either.

Interestingly, my first tattoo, which I got when I was eighteen, was of the Irish claddagh cross with my middle name, Faith, down the middle of the cross. That, in itself, is funny, considering that my middle name came from a baby book (not because of any religious fervor on my parents' part), and I had had a hard time saying my middle name as a child (I would say "face," not Faith). I do love my middle name, and I now have "Faith" pictures and mementos everywhere in my house, in my car, and even in my office. But when I got that tattoo at eighteen, I wasn't a religious person. I had always been a very spiritual person, but I did not consider myself religious.

It wasn't until a few years later when I truly started to believe in something bigger than myself. At twenty-two years old, I became pregnant. At the time, I wasn't married or even in a relationship, and I had no clue what I was going to do. I prayed and prayed on what I should do, until God made the decision for me when I ended up having a miscarriage. Now, don't get me wrong, that was a horrible and very emotional experience, and I hate that it happened. But it happened because God knew that, as a single twenty-two-year-old, I was in no position to become a mother, nor raise a child on my own. I thank God every day for making that decision for me. That is another reason why I believe he waited almost twenty years to give me Logan!

Fast forward to meeting my husband, finding the perfect career, getting married, and trying to have a baby. When we were trying to have Logan, we had to see a fertility specialist, to just give us a kick start in the process. One day, on my way to have testing done at the fertility clinic, I was the victim of road rage. In all honesty, I had accidentally cut someone off in the fast lane. It was one of those situations where you check your mirror and look over your shoulder, you move over, and suddenly someone is there. Well, anyway, I got out of this person's way, and they proceeded to return the favor by cutting me off. I was flabbergasted. At that point, I could tell the person was extremely aggressive, and I tried every-thing to get away from them. He cut me off a second time and I ended up doing a 360 on the thruway into morning rush-hour traffic. Miraculously, I managed *not* to hit any other cars, and I missed the guardrail, which I stopped mere inches from. God had been watching over me that morning.

After conceiving, everything about my pregnancy had been status quo. The only concern had been Logan's slightly enlarged kidney, which we were told was a common abnormality—no big deal. Once again, God intervened on the day of our last ultrasound. (I know I already shared this in a previous chapter, but it's worth mentioning again here). We were almost ten minutes late to that appointment, which was going to be the last ultrasound before Logan's due date of December 18. If we had been *one more minute late* to that ultrasound, they would have canceled our appointment. And, as it turned out, the doctor who found the fluid on Logan's brain had just started a week prior and had specialized in this type of medical issue. Then came the hemorrhage, and Logan was born via emergency C-section. My faith once again saw me through when the doctor told us that Logan had a deadly platelet disorder. I knew that God had not given me my baby at forty years old to take him away from me. Logan had stayed in the NICU for five days and was tested for everything, but they couldn't find anything wrong. They called him the "Miracle Baby" of Albany Med.

When Logan was later diagnosed with a glioblastoma, the doctors said there wasn't much they could do and that we should prepare ourselves for the worst. Again, I couldn't help but feel that God had brought Logan to us for a reason, so I put out the call for help on social media and asked for prayers for our baby. At first, I didn't share about Logan's diagnosis, I just said that we needed prayers. Sure enough, the prayers came through, and three days later, the doctors told us that Logan had a congenital glioblastoma, which was reason to be "cautiously optimistic."

Throughout the entire time, Logan was going through treatment, everything we had been through had helped me reconnect with God and believe in the power of prayer. Sometimes we need to face the worst things in life before we can find the best things about life. There is no doubt that Logan chose my husband and me to be his parents for a reason, and I know that all the connections and "coincidences" that have happened have been God's work. I say "coincidences" because, honestly, I don't believe in coincidences. I truly believe that everything happens for a reason, and I believe that God gave us Logan because He knew that we would be strong enough financially, mentally, emotionally, and spiritually to be able to handle the situation and overcome every obstacle that would be placed in our way. I also know that Logan chose me to be his mom because I have a big mouth! In a good way, though, because he knew that I wouldn't be afraid to speak up and fight for him. For example, one of Logan's first occupational therapists (OTs) during early intervention was a very nice person and a good OT. She was so gentle with Logan, but sometimes too gentle. I ended up reaching out to our early intervention coordinator and requesting a new OT. We wanted someone who wasn't going to coddle Logan, someone who would push him, someone who had a "no pain, no gain" mentality. We hadn't gotten as far as we had by letting Logan stop therapy because he was mad, sick, or in pain. That wasn't how my husband or I had been brought up, and coddling him sure as hell was not how our son would succeed and overcome his delays. If we were going to fight for our son, our son was going to learn how to push through and fight on his own!

I went to church with my father-in-law, Butch, and Kevin's late grandmother, Sheila (God, I miss that woman), throughout Logan's treatment. After Kevin and I were married, I had gone to church with his father every week, and when my in-laws moved out of state, I began going with Sheila on Saturday afternoons. Later, when Logan was first born, I would take him with me. I wasn't a "regular" at church, but when I did go, the parish was very supportive and always asked about Logan and would pray with and over me and my family. It was funny because Butch and Sheila sat in different spots in church and went on different days, so I was exposed to so many great people of all ages and backgrounds. An older couple that sat in front of me and Butch were both retired teachers. One day, the wife said something to me that resonated, and I still carry her words with me to this day. She said, "Life is like a river, and you are the water. You must go through the hills, the valleys, and the bends. But remember to keep flowing, just like water." This goes for anything in life. Be like water—keep going and let things flow off of you!

But I still found myself needing something more. I needed to be closer to God, to understand God, and to learn more about the Bible and who these people were that we call the "Father, the Son, and the Holy Spirit." I needed to learn more so that I could raise my son in the church and teach him about the Catholic faith. I needed to be able to explain to Logan how we had believed, and how strangers had prayed for him. I needed to do this for my son, and for all of the people who had prayed (and continue to pray) for our family. Most importantly, I needed to do it for myself, so I could be closer with God and have faith in the world and this life. So I decided to receive my communion and confirmation, and I started attending Rite of Christian Initiation of Adults (RCIA) classes. This was a feat because Logan was still going through treatment at the time, and Kevin and I were both working full-time. Thankfully, Kevin and my mother were willing to help with Logan on the nights when I had class.

At the Easter Vigil in 2018, I received my first communion and confirmation at St. Joseph's Church in Scotia, surrounded by my closest loved ones. My dear friend, Bridget, had been my sponsor through my journey to Catholicism, and I had chosen the confirmation name of "Bridget" in honor of my Irish heritage and in honor of Saint Brigit, the patron saint of infants who is also known for her faith and her unwavering trust in God. My in-laws had driven up from North Carolina to be there for me as I got confirmed, and I had Deacon Stephen Lape and Father Peter Russo by my side. My mother and stepfather were also there, and of course, my husband and Logan. I was also grateful to have my BFF, Colby Enides, who is not religious, and nevertheless sat through the two-hour mass and even received communion to support me. Having everyone's support meant so much to me. They supported me and my decisions, and ultimately, this affected Logan. Even though he didn't understand what was going on, having happy and loving people around him in the presence of God was a positive experience for him (and me). It meant the world to me to show Logan what it means to be supported and surrounded by loved ones. Logan will always be the only thing that matters, and everything I do is for him, in the eyes of God.

There had continued to be coincidences throughout our journey, and any time we had a curveball thrown at us, I would just sit back (okay, not very patiently) and wait for the situation to work itself out. (I would say that things work out in our favor about 90 percent of the time. And when things *don't* work out, if we wait just a little bit longer, they usually do. I always get my way! I know this sounds obnoxious, but I know what is best for my son, and if I ask for it, fight for it, and pray for it, it works out for the best for Logan and our family. I always get what I want, and if I don't, it's because I didn't want it badly enough or because it wasn't meant to be.) In one such "coincidence," one of my church sponsors turned out to also be a fellow Rotarian whom I had known for years. This made me feel extra comfortable, as this was

Kevin's family's church. I hadn't grown up in church or in that area, and I didn't know many people, except for a couple of my father-in-law's associates at church. So, it was really nice to know someone from my own network.

I will forever believe that Logan is here for a reason and that he chose us to be his parents for a reason. He knew we would get him through treatment, we would help him beat cancer, and we will see him through all of the other obstacles we now face. We continue to have faith in Logan and in the higher power of God. We believe that everything will work out for the best and He will overcome. Now, if someone could just teach me patience, we'd all be better off! Needless to say, my middle name is Faith for a reason...because my faith sees me through, even when my patience and my strength are being challenged!

CHAPTER

13

SEPTEMBER IS CHILDHOOD Cancer Awareness month, and I will *always* "Be Bold, Go Gold," as the slogan goes. But for my family, September 2018 was especially significant because we hit the trifecta! I got to meet Robin Roberts from "Good Morning America" and share Logan's story, the Union College hockey team "adopted" Logan and made him an honorary team member, and Logan rang the bell signifying the end of his treatment.

A year earlier, I had made a Facebook video stating that my goal was to meet Robin Roberts and go on "Good Morning America" ("GMA") to share Logan's story. Robin Roberts is a cancer survivor herself, and I just felt a connection with her. Then, in September 2018, with the help of our friends at the local Channel 10 affiliates, I was given tickets to see a live taping of "GMA." *So cool!* Unfortunately, September is also hurricane season, and the weather had taken a turn for the worst, so our taping got bumped to the new "GMA Day" (now called "GMA3") daytime show because the morning hosts were busy tracking and reporting on the storm. *Hey, I'll take it.* So, with two of the original board members of the Logan Strong™ Foundation, we drove to New York City, spent the night, and went to see "GMA Day" hosted by Michael Strahan and Sara Haines. As luck would have it, we were walking to the doors of the GMA studio just as Robin Roberts was walking out from the other door toward her car. *What?!* Can you guess what I did next? Yep, I ran up to her as calmly as I could and introduced myself. After briefly sharing Logan's story, I handed her a bag of goodies that I had prepared and had planned to leave at the studio in the hope that someone would get it to her. I never imagined I would be able to give it to her myself! (Robin, if you're reading this, do you remember that crazy lady in gold who talked about #LoganStrong? Yep, that was me! Can I come on your show now?) Meeting Robin Roberts and sharing Logan's story had been my goal for the past year, and I did it! Anything else that happened that day was just a bonus. Watching them tape "GMA Day" was so much fun. The three of us sat in the front row, proudly wearing our gold shirts and ribbons for Childhood Cancer Awareness month.

The very next day we were to have another amazing experience. There is a local organization that partners cancer families with local sports teams who "adopt" a pediatric cancer patient and that child becomes their "mascot" for the season. We had been nominated through an old business acquaintance of mine in late 2017 and were asked what sports we liked. We said, of course, hockey or baseball. At the time, it was the middle of winter and SUNY Albany (our local state college) baseball season was over, so they suggested the RPI men's hockey team. You may be familiar with rivalries like the Yankees versus the Red Sox. Well, RPI was the rival of Union, which is our favorite local college hockey team, so we knew a match with RPI wasn't in the stars. But the organization didn't have any contacts at Union, so I did what I do best—I connected them with the Union College men's hockey team, and that year Logan was adopted by the team. We were ecstatic! My husband had been going to Union College hockey games for as long as he could remember. We had season tickets every year, and one of the coaches was married to our contact and friend at the local television station. I will never forget the day when Logan was adopted by Union. We walked in the back door of the locker room and the "boys" (as I called them, and still do) were doing their thing, watching TV, chatting, and messing around. As they gathered around us, we shared Logan's story and they were so completely enamored with our son and all he had been through. They were genuinely interested and concerned. I was so touched to see that a bunch of young college athletes could feel so connected with my son. It was one of the most beautiful experiences. Before we left, they showered us with Union College hockey gear, including shirts, sweatshirts, jerseys, hats, and pucks. They even gave Logan his own locker and jersey number. At the time, Logan was still getting sick regularly because of the lingering chemo and feeding issues, and at one point, he got sick in one of the guys' lockers. I thought to myself, *That's gotta be good luck, right?!* Since that day, we have become so close with the boys, especially their captain, Cole Maier, and their assistant captain, Ryan Walker. In fact, we still talk to them to this day. All of the boys even wore #LoganStrong stickers on their helmets that season.

Shortly after meeting the Union hockey team, we celebrated Logan's bell-ringing. Ringing the bell marks a milestone in someone's cancer treatment. It signifies the end, but it's also a beginning. It's a new lease on life, a fresh start, a chance to wipe the slate clean. In our case, it was truly a new beginning, but a beginning with a sense of loss. We had lost almost two years of our son's life, two years of development, and two years of normal milestones.

Originally, Logan had been set to do eight rounds of outpatient chemotherapy, but on August 14, 2018 (the day before my husband's birthday), we had gone in for Logan's last chemo of round six when Dr. Weintraub shocked us with the news that that would be his last treatment. I was confused. *Really? Why? Was something wrong?* Nope, it was just the opposite. Dr. Weintraub explained to us that she was part of a national brain tumor board, and she had been discussing Logan's treatment with the board since day one. (Think of it as an advisory board or a weekly sales meeting of sorts. Can you tell I'm in sales?!) Because Logan's cancer was so rare, he was a case study for the medical world, and what they were learning from his cancer was going to help others fight and survive this awful disease. At the board's last advisory meeting, when they discussed Logan's case, they agreed unanimously that they felt they had overtreated him at that point. *What?! Really?! Overtreated?!* And to top it all off, they were confident that the cancer would never return. Plus, Dr. Weintraub had learned that because Logan had certain genetic markers, if the tumor did come back, there was a new drug on the market that attacked this specific mutation. Science works, people! They not only cured my son of cancer (you know, the cancer they had said there was nothing they could do about, the cancer they said he would never survive), but now they were saying that it wouldn't come back!

Although Logan technically finished treatment in August, we wanted to make his bell-ringing totally official with the removal of his port. Typically, they don't remove a child's port for about six months after treatment, but our little rock star did so well that the doctors only made him keep it in for a month. His port surgery was postponed a week because Logan's blood counts weren't where they wanted them to be for sedation and surgery, which totally sucked—it was just one more thing to wait for, but we obviously understood. So, we scheduled his port removal and bell-ringing for Monday, September 24, 2018.

Leading up to the big day, I had so many mixed emotions. Having a child with cancer and going through continuous treatment was all I had known. I would always worry if his tumor might come back. I would always worry about whether his development will ever catch up. I would always wonder what my son's life will be like in the future. *Will there be more side effects from the treatment? Will he ever walk? Will he ever talk? Will he ever eat enough by mouth so we can get rid of the G-tube?* Fighting for Logan's life was all I knew how to do, and ringing the bell meant we were really on our own— for everything! It meant our new normal. It meant making *all* of Logan's life decisions on our own. *What?! How the hell are we going to do that?!*

It may seem counterintuitive, but ringing the bell meant that the "easy" part was over and the "hard" part was about to begin. At least with treatment, we had been given timelines. We had been told how long each round would last, what to expect, and how Logan may act or feel. Even with the major brain surgeries, we were told the risks, how long the surgery would last, how he would be after, how we should care for him, and what the next steps would be. Through the year and a half of Logan's cancer treatment, there was always a plan with an outcome, and as long as we followed those steps in the plan, we would achieve our goal for Logan to be cancer-free and treatment-free. But now that his treatment was officially over, we were in totally new territory—and it was all up to us now.

My goal had been to get Logan through treatment with my breast milk, and literally, almost to the day, I was able to do that for him. I felt that the nutrition from my breast milk would be a huge benefit to his fight and his overall health, and the doctors agreed that it had helped him through treatment. Breast milk provides the ideal nutrition for infants because it's said to have the perfect mix of vitamins, protein, and fat—everything a baby needs to grow, and it's all provided in a form that is more easily digested than infant formula. Breast milk also contains antibodies that help babies fight off viruses and bacteria, which was especially important in Logan's case.

Getting my son through treatment was all I knew. And I did it. *We did it.* Yes, I was excited for this next phase in his life (and our lives) in which we could focus on his development, but I worried if I was strong enough, if my husband was strong enough, if Logan was strong enough. There were so many questions racing through my head. By that point, I was completely exhausted, burned-out, drained, shattered, and broken. *How was I going to continue?* I knew that whenever I started to notice these feelings of defeat, I just needed a rest. I needed a minute to collect my thoughts, regain my strength, and put one foot in front of the other. And that's exactly what I did. My middle name isn't Faith for no reason! *We've got this! Let's go!*

So when it came to Logan's bell-ringing, you would think I would be ecstatic, but it wasn't quite that simple. I don't know if anyone can ever understand the emotional roller coaster of being a cancer mom unless you've been through it—and I hope you never have to go through that. It's not a cakewalk, it's not all sunshine and roses. It fucking sucks. But I'm not a quitter, neither is my husband, and we all know that Logan isn't either. The level of emotional, physical, and mental trauma we had gone through was insane. PTSD is real.

To commemorate Logan's bell-ringing, we had new T-shirts made with the "Puck Cancer" logo and his treatment dates in the puck (3/8/17–9/24/18), and of course, we had a shirt specially made for Logan that said, "I smacked the puck out of cancer." In hindsight, I feel so badly for the patients who were getting treatment that day because I created a major event with this. The hallway of the Melodies Center was lined on both sides with our closest family, friends, and supporters, not to mention the news channels and a couple of reporters. Logan's story was a big deal locally—well, because I made it so, selfishly for prayers for my son but also selflessly to spread awareness and hope and faith in miracles. So, to the families that were there receiving treatment that day, I want to extend my sincerest apologies. I was in my own little world at that moment, and it was selfish of me not to think of the hard time you were going through. Even as we were celebrating, I felt guilty for all our friends who were still fighting. I felt guilty for the friends I had met who had children who had lost their battles. It was part guilt, part fear, part excitement, and part gratitude. And honestly, I sometimes wonder how we got so lucky to have our baby be the miracle. I still cry whenever I think about this because it's such a bag of mixed emotions. My therapist had warned me about this, the emotional roller coaster that would be on the horizon when Logan's treatment was officially done. It had been such a long road and we had seen the good, the bad, and the ugly. And yes, while I knew Logan deserved it (and we deserved it), the emotions at that time were so hard to put into words.

When it came time to ring the bell, Logan wanted nothing to do with it, which was totally ironic because the kid loved (and still loves) to bang on the drums. Kevin held him while I helped him with the gong, and oh boy, he did not like it!

And that was the end of treatment. The next day, I went on the local news to share our story and the update about the end of Logan's treatment and what was next—which I was totally clueless about. *What was I going to do next?*

On Logan's second birthday, he was officially baptized in the church. His godmother is my best friend, Colby, and his godfather is Dan, one of Kevin's best friends. They had both been with us not only throughout each of our lives but also during Logan's treatment and beyond. We were so blessed to not only be done with treatment but to also be able to baptize him officially in the church on his actual birthday. We had a small family party afterward to celebrate both milestones.

In early December, we had a combination end of treatment/birthday party. The best part was that we had help from another local organization whose mission is to give cancer families the "best day ever," and they planned everything for this celebration. We obviously went with a hockey theme for this celebration since Logan "smacked the puck out of cancer." One of the best parts about that day was that almost the entire Union College men's hockey team showed up to celebrate with us! The kids at the party were starstruck because most of them looked at the team as local celebrities, and they played games with the kids, danced, and just had a great time! On that day, I just fell in love with those boys so much more. They didn't have to do those things; they did them because they wanted to. Each year, for Logan's birthday, we also do a fundraiser. For the first year, we had asked people to donate to the Melodies Center in Logan's name, and for his second birthday, we did a toy drive and asked our guests to bring new toys for us to donate to Albany Medical Center. After Logan's party, we began looking to the year ahead—our first year fully cancer-free and treatment-free!

CHAPTER

14

BY THE BEGINNING of the next year, we were trying to find our new normal as we were finally living at home, not having several doctors' appointments a week, and not having to worry anymore about chemotherapy. Both my husband and I were back to work full-time. I have always been a hard worker; I get that from my parents. So being back to work full-time not only rebuilt my confidence but also helped me find myself again. Kevin felt the same way too. Although he didn't have as much guilt as I did about working and not being at the hospital, he could now work and be a dad without feeling like he was missing out on much or feeling guilty if he couldn't be there for us. For me, going back to work reinforced that life didn't always have to be about fighting cancer and living in the hospital. I was able to be a mom *and* a business professional, *and* I could still be *me*, not just a cancer mom. I found passion in my work again, and I now had a more meaningful reason to do what I do, helping protect people from the "what-whens" in life, not just the "what-ifs," because I had just lived through the worst possible "what-when." I was also working on building the Logan Strong™ Foundation, and for the first time in a long while, we even had time to enjoy some of the activities we had missed out on over the past two years. Kevin started playing hockey again and I became more active in my Rotary chapter. Not to mention that we were caring for our special-needs child—oh, and somewhere in there we were also trying to keep our marriage healthy and happy! To say we were busy would be a massive understatement, and thank God we had two nannies to help us with Logan along the way. He was now receiving early intervention services through the county, plus he had physical therapy (PT), occupational therapy (OT), special education (yep, that's a therapy), music therapy, speech/feeding therapy, and lessons with a teacher of the deaf (no, he wasn't deaf, but this was to help him learn sign language and communicate). And he still had one to two doctors' appointments a month. In hindsight, I'm grateful we were so busy during this time because it created a structure we could follow as we transitioned into our new normal. We didn't have time to worry or stress over what we had just been through. Instead, we focused on our future, on Logan's future, on his development, and on our goals as a family. It was never going to be "normal," but anything was better than what we had just lived through!

On February 13, 2019, Logan was scheduled to have his six-month scan. Up to this point, he had needed a scan every three months until he had graduated to six-month scans when he had finished treatment in August. And to top it off, the next day, February 14, would be exactly six months since Logan's last chemo treatment. As you can imagine, my anxiety was high! But more importantly, my *scanxiety* was through the roof! What's the difference between anxiety and scanxiety? Anxiety—at least how I perceive it—is usually about what might happen or what is about to happen. But scanxiety is about what *did* happen, and it's not so much about worrying as it is about *remembering*. It's reliving the fears from the results of his first MRI when they found the tumor. It's remembering what the worst-case scenario was, and that it had already happened. With scanxiety, it's like my body and my heart were right back in those horrible moments—it's real, and it became even more real now that we were done with treatment.

On the day of his six-month MRI, I didn't want to cry because I was afraid I wouldn't stop. I was beyond anxious, nervous, scared—and all the other emotions—as we waited for Logan to come out of his MRI. I've since lost count of how many MRIs he's had or how many times he's been sedated, but I will tell you that this day was *by far* the *hardest* of them all. He had kicked and screamed the entire time we were in the pre-op room. Logan's developmental pediatrician, Dr. Lucas, had warned us that this would happen because the older Logan got the more aware he would be when he was at the doctor's office or hospital and he would be more likely to react defiantly. The poor kid had been poked and prodded more times than I care to even remember, and he *hated* it!

I didn't tell my husband how nervous I was, and he didn't tell me how nervous he was either. We were trying to be strong for one another, so in the days leading up to the scan, we both buried ourselves in our work and our extracurriculars. The waiting room of the imaging department had become a second home for us (outside of Logan's hospital room), and we each had our favorite spots to sit. On the day of his six-month scan, after Logan was in the doctor's hands, I went across the street to Starbucks to get us coffee and breakfast. I came back to find Kevin reading articles on his phone about hockey or motorcycle racing. I had brought my laptop, so I spent the time getting caught up on emails and other work. Neither of us spoke, but we were both thinking the same things. *What if the tumor came back? How would we get through this again? No, that's not an option. We need to stay positive. It's not going to come back, ever!*

When we got the good news that Logan's scan looked great and that it was all clear, I just broke down in tears. (To this day, my eyes always well up from relief of the good news whenever we take him in for an MRI. That scanxiety never really leaves you!) As I was crying, Dr. Weintraub asked why I was so upset. I knew part of my response was simply a release after holding in all of my scanxiety, but I was also worried because the next day was exactly six months post-treatment, and I knew that some of the chemotherapies Logan had received would stay in his system for six months because I had asked Dr. Weintraub about that earlier. I'm obviously not a medical professional, so I didn't know if this meant that Logan would end up needing more chemo. *Did this mean that the tumor would come back? Did it mean that he would have a different cancer?* So many "what-ifs" ran through my head. But we got through it—and we continue to get through it—because we stay positive and do not focus on the "what-ifs." Instead, we focus on the "what-whens," including the positive moments in life! When we got in the car to go home after the scan, Kevin told me his stomach had been in knots all day. In a strange way, it was comforting to know that he had been just as nervous as I was!

In those days, Logan was a real *terdler* (as we liked to call him). He was moody, he would cry for no reason (or we just didn't know why he was crying because he wasn't talking yet and he couldn't communicate his needs), and we were noticing some regression in certain behaviors. He was banging his head more often (again we didn't know why, or what was wrong, because he couldn't tell us). He was also exhibiting some aggressive behaviors, including literally attacking us (he would attack me more often than Kevin) for no apparent reason. During his feeds, he would either hit us or try to bite us, which not only made it extremely difficult to get his feeds done but it also tested our patience. Being constantly attacked, bitten, hit, grabbed, or scratched by your child definitely tests your patience, which is a Catch-22 because children mimic adult behaviors, so if we got upset or lost our patience, Logan would learn those same behaviors. At times, it would become a tag-team effort. If Kevin or I lost our patience, the other one would step in to help. We still do this to this day, and trust me, it's easier said than done at times! A lot of this was a result of his brain injury, but some of it was just normal toddler stuff. (The "terrible twos" are no joke—especially when your kid has a traumatic brain injury!) I wasn't used to "normal." All I had known of motherhood had been wrapped up in Logan's cancer treatment. Give me chemo, give me weeks at a time of living in the hospital, give me an eight-hour surgery...*that* I can handle; toddlers, not so much! It totally sucks that my "normal" had been living in the hospital and fighting for my son's life. Who waits to get married later in life, has their first child at forty, and signs up for this shit?! It fucking sucked; I'm not going to sugarcoat it. I still have days when I am beyond angry and hurt that these were the cards we were dealt. But then I also have days when I can rally and say to myself, *OK, we can do this. What's next? We've got this.* I know in my heart that Logan was meant to be our son. I know that this whole situation was meant to happen. I do not question that; I just don't have to like it all the time. So when I say that the day of Logan's six-month MRI was the hardest day I had had in a while, I mean it. And I would not wish this journey on anyone.

Yes, Logan was cancer-free and treatment-free at this point, but we now had a whole different road ahead of us! Not only had my son been born with cancer, but because of the cancer, he had to have a part of his brain removed which was now affecting his development. That was a tough pill to swallow. *Would this get any easier over time?* Maybe, but the worst-case scenario would always be in the backs of our minds. Even though his developmental pediatrician had given us the green light and was hopeful that Logan would catch up and develop normally, I wanted my "normal" baby now! I wanted Logan to grow up so we could put all of this behind us. We had been through the worst, and now I just wanted to believe that things could finally get better. I was done waiting for our "normal" life as a "normal" family. I was angry, sad, uneasy—you name it, I was feeling it. But thank God my kid is cute! Like, really fucking cute! Not only had his hair started to grow back, but he was also starting to lose his baby face. He was coming into his own personality because he was no longer living in the hospital and could experience life as a "normal" kid (as "normal" as possible, that is). Around this time, we had gotten him a plastic Starbucks cup that looked exactly like the paper cups I would get when I ordered my coffee, and he would pretend he was sipping out of it. The kid wouldn't eat or drink by mouth, but he would pretend to mimic Mommy drinking her coffee. *Unbelievable!* He also wouldn't go anywhere without his little music box. I literally purchased them in bulk because he had to have one everywhere he went. And God forbid if one broke—and they did, because he liked to throw them. He would carry his box around like an eighties boom box; it was adorable. I'm not exaggerating when I say that he had over a dozen of these little music boxes at any given time. There was one in my car, another in Kevin's car, one in the diaper bag, one in his bedroom, another in his toy box, and of course, I had a secret backup stash! And I can't forget his hearing aids...his audiologist surprised us by putting hockey stick emblems on them. *Super cute!* They're part of Logan's signature look! Logan has hearing loss from the chemotherapy, which is a typical side effect from treatment. They don't know if it's permanent, and it's monitored with an ABR (auditory brainstem response test, which tells how the inner ear, called the cochlea, and the brain pathways for hearing are working) that he receives during his annual MRI checks. Now every time he gets sized for a new pair, it's assumed that we just keep getting the hockey sticks.

CHAPTER
15

ON MARCH 7, 2019, the day before Logan's two-year cancerversay, I found myself sitting in the cafeteria at Albany Medical Center. But, unlike so many other occasions in the hospital cafeteria, this time I didn't have to rush to an appointment or back to Logan's room to see if something was going on. Nope, on his second cancerversary, I was in the hospital cafeteria because I wanted to get some writing done for the Logan Strong™ blog—plus it was Wednesday, and that meant it was turkey day! There I was, sitting at my laptop, with my Starbucks coffee in hand (another addiction I blame on living at Albany Med; my only escape from hospital life was walking across the street to get my triple grande skinny vanilla latte most mornings). Yes, I drove over twenty miles to get writing done, and to get a turkey sandwich (in my defense, I also had some donations to drop off). It was two years later and I was still scrambling for "me time," and I still loved those damn turkey sandwiches. Some things will never change. Do you know what else will never change? Every year on this day, I say, "One year ago, two years ago, my life changed." I will *never* lose sight of how much this journey has affected our family!

Not only does each cancerversary bring up lots of memories, but they also prompt me to reflect on how far we have truly come! Every year, the weeks surrounding Logan's diagnosis day are always hard, and the worst part is the time between his birthday and March 8 (his diagnosis date). That time period always wrecks me because in that first year, this was the only time in our lives when things were "normal." We didn't know yet what we would be in for—we had no clue how our lives were about to be flipped upside down. We were just thrilled to be new parents, and we were falling totally in love with our new baby boy.

This particular anniversary was bittersweet for us because our friend, Gracie, had gotten to ring the bell on that same day! As you now know, the bell-ringing signifies the end of a cancer patient's treatment. Our girl, Gracie, had been diagnosed with leukemia on her tenth birthday and had been going through treatment for almost three years. Now she was ringing the bell on Logan's cancerversary! Every family's experience is unique, but I had a pretty good idea of how Gracie and her family felt on that day. There is, of course, relief and happiness, but you also know that your cancer journey will always be part of who you are. I've said it before, and I'll say it again, hearing the words, "Your child has cancer!" smacks you in the face like a Mack truck! I would much rather have heard those words about myself. It's hard, it hurts, it's surreal, and it's bittersweet.

The first anniversary of his diagnosis had been exciting. I thought, *Oh my God, this is amazing! We made it a year! They had told me my son wouldn't survive, and now we have made it a year!* But on the second anniversary, my thoughts were more like, *Holy crap, I've been doing this for two years... This fucking sucks! This is our life. Ugh. Another day. Another month. Another year.* I know some people probably thought I should just be happy that my son was cancer-free and treatment-free two years later. Here's the thing: I was *beyond* grateful, and I will forever be grateful that my son has beaten cancer and has defied all the odds. And yes, I'm grateful that he's *alive*! But in reality, two years later, I still had PTSD, and I was constantly grieving the loss of having a "normal" child with "normal" milestones. Yes, I am strong. I don't like being upset, and I don't accept defeat. That's why my son has made it this far, because of my husband and me. We don't accept the worst-case scenario, and we believe in the power of prayer and positive thinking. Logan dying was *never an option*! It's still *not an option*, but it's *always* in the back of my head.

I wasn't really talking to anyone about how I felt because I didn't want to be judged, and quite honestly, I figured no one could truly understand what I was going through. Any time I would tell someone how I was feeling—that I wished Logan was walking, talking, or eating—the first response I always got was, "Well, he's cancer-free!" *No shit!* I knew this, but that didn't mean I didn't mourn the loss of "normal." Wanting "normal" had *nothing* to do with being grateful; it was about wanting what I had dreamed about my entire life, having a healthy baby that would grow and develop "normally." I just wanted my kid to walk, talk, and eat like any other almost two-and-a-half-year-old would. By this time, Logan wasn't walking yet, and he hadn't taken his first steps until that past August. Can you imagine what it's like to go out to a birthday party, family event, or sporting event and have to keep your toddler in their stroller because they can't walk?! *It fucking sucks!* Logan had turned two that past November and him still not being able to walk broke my heart; it killed me that at two years old my child wasn't walking. But do you know what I did? I made sure his therapy sessions still happened, I practiced walking with him, and we did exercises and everything else necessary to help with his development. I hated it, but I fucking did what was necessary and what was best for my kid—and I *always* will! Yes, I did not doubt that Logan would catch up with walking, talking, and eating, but that doesn't mean it didn't hurt or that I didn't want "normal."

What I really want people to understand is that PTSD is real, and mourning the loss of something you had always wanted but don't have is real—and it sucks. I knew I had every right to feel this way, and I didn't need a pep talk. I didn't need to hear, "Well, he's cute," or, "He's cancer-free," or "He's this or that." Sometimes I just needed someone to say, "Yeah, you know what? It does suck. What can I do to help? How are *you* doing?" I thank God that we had such an amazing support system, and there were a few people whom I could rely on to be there for me in the way I needed.

And while it truly does take a village to raise a child—and

it certainly took a village to get us through those first two years—there was one person in our lives who turned out to be not quite what she had seemed. To be honest, I struggled with whether I wanted to share this part of our story in the book because the last thing I want to do is bash another person, but in the end, I felt it was important to share because it, unfortunately, shows how selfish some people are and how lonely this journey can really be at times! Back in January 2018, I had returned to work full-time, and we were lucky enough to have found an amazing nanny during this time. I had known her for years and she had come back into our lives just before Logan's first birthday. She and I had been business associates for years, and while we butted heads, we always had the same goal in mind. We used to joke that because we both had very type A personalities, she was A- and I was A+. We got along great, even though she was very overbearing and could cross the line at times. At the end of the day, it was always about Logan and what was best for him, and she was so good with him! She was a pit bull whenever we would go to events. She was the one who would always tell people to back off, and she wouldn't let anyone get too close to him. It was great. She also had our permission to post on social media about all the happenings throughout the day because we had gained a strong following on Facebook with Logan's journey, and we knew it was important to keep people updated and informed about what the day-to-day looked like. She would post things about his therapies, his gains, and the funny or cute things he did. She sometimes overshared a bit by not only posting about his bowel movements, but she also created her own hashtag, making it about her and Logan. More and more, it was about her and what she did, as if Logan were *her* son.

I know that in her heart she had Logan's best interest in mind, and I really am grateful for the two years she gave us. I hope she reads this and knows that if it hadn't been for her, I wouldn't have been able to go back to work, and Logan probably wouldn't have come as far as he did in those two years she was with us. Hand to God, I am truly grateful for her. *But* she did me wrong, and she did *us* wrong. I trusted her, probably too much. She would take Logan to his doctors' appointments and therapies, she ran errands with him, she even invited us to her family vacations and would watch Logan so Kevin and I could have date nights. She was so giving, and while she thinks I took advantage of her—which I don't think I did—I will admit that I did take her for granted. How could I have known any differently? I was a new mom, and a cancer mom, who had just spent the better part of six months living in the hospital while my son had been fighting for his life. And once I had an opportunity for some sort of normalcy, I took it! Hindsight is always twenty-twenty.

What happened in late fall 2019 was, for lack of a better word, disgusting. What she did was so far out of line that I don't know how she could sleep at night. See, we had trusted her with scheduling Logan's therapies at home, and it turned out that one of his therapists at the time had hired her out from underneath us. Yep, you read that right. While part of me blames the therapist because she had been providing a service to our family and was bound by HIPAA (and you can bet your ass we fired that therapist!), I also blame our nanny for going behind our backs to not only look for another job but to *use one of the services that was helping our son*! To say we were *livid* would be putting it nicely. I can still feel my heart pounding whenever I think about it today; it still pisses me off. *How could she do that to our family? How could she do that to a kid, and especially a special-needs kid? How could she do that to a friend?* That's some shady shit! Needless to say, the next few weeks were very uncomfortable and awkward as she had agreed to work until the end of the year (almost, she ended up giving me a week's notice during the busiest time of year for my business). I also found out that she had told one of my employees that she was quitting before she told me. Her words were, "I wanted to tell you first in case Jen is in a bad mood on Monday." *What?! Who does that?!*

But one of the things I've learned from our journey with Logan is that there is always some bit of good that can be found in every experience. And in this case, the bright side was that losing our nanny brought about a change that I didn't even know I had needed. By this time I had been an independent agent with Aflac for almost seven years, four of which had been in management. Now I had to make the decision to either continue with management and find another nanny or step down from management and take care of my son. It was (and still is) very hard to find someone to take care of Logan because they would have to be "on" all the time. It involves tube feeds and therapies, headbanging, and other aggressive behaviors. It takes a special person. So I needed to decide if I wanted to stay in management and devote my time to a team of agents to help them build their careers or manage my son's needs and be there for him. I chose the latter. Logan was by far more important. It was a hard decision because I loved (and still do love) my job, and I enjoyed meeting people and helping others. Plus, my work had allowed me to have a sense of normalcy. You know, get up, get your kid ready for school or day care, drop him off (in our case, the nanny would bring him to school), go to work, come home, and be a mom at night. It was so wonderfully normal—for a time.

But because this happened with our nanny, I realized that I had been hiding. I had gone from one extreme (cancer mom) to another (working mom), and I needed to find a balance. My husband agreed that stepping down would be the right thing for our family, and financially we could afford to do so. So I made the hard decision to step down from management. And let me just say how amazing it is to work with Aflac. What other company would let you decide to demote yourself, and then when you're ready, let you promote yourself again? I am super blessed with this career. When I called my boss and told her I needed to step down, I was crying my eyes out as I explained to her why and what had happened. It was a pivotal moment for me, and thankfully, she respected my decision to put my son first.

As of January 1, 2020, I was just an agent! No quotas, no mandatory meetings, no training other agents... I was able to control my schedule, and my time was mine. It worked out great! Kevin would bring Logan to school in the morning, and I would work for a few hours before picking him up from school. Most days, he would have therapy or an occasional doctor's appointment afterward. I finally had *freedom*! I could be a cancer mom *and* a working mom... Who knew?!

So, as much as what our nanny did was shady as fuck (yep, I said it), it happened for a reason, and I thank her for doing that so I could find the balance that I had been missing. And, once again, the universe had my back because I stepped down from management in January 2020, and then in March 2020 the COVID pandemic hit. When the world shut down, I didn't have to worry about anyone but Logan—not a quota, not training new agents, not mandatory meetings—just being Mommy to Logan.

CHAPTER
16

BY MARCH 8, 2020, Logan's third cancerversary, he was doing A–M–A–Z–I–N–G. He was sleeping through the night (which we'd never had a problem with) and he was taking naps without any fuss. We had him on a schedule of feeds, therapies, school, naps, play, etc. Consistency and keeping to a schedule was so good for his development and his temperament. He was also understanding what we were saying; even if he couldn't talk or use sign language very well, he totally understood whatever we asked or told him.

My favorite part of our journey up to that point—besides Logan surviving and kicking cancer's ass, of course—was that he started walking. In fact, he was running! The first time he started walking, he was going so fast, it was like he just had to figure out how to get up on his feet and keep his balance, and then he just took off from there. He never wanted to stop walking, and to this day, he loves to be on the move, whether it's going for a ride in the car, playing in his ball pit in the basement, jumping on his trampoline outside, or going for a walk (most times without his stroller now). And he absolutely loves the wind in his face (and hair). My goal had been to have Logan walking by the time he started pre-K, and sure enough, in late August 2019, he started walking just before school started in September. To this day, I love when people say, "Look at him go," or, "He has you on your toes," or, "Run, Bubba, run!" And every time I look at them and say, "And they told me he would never walk."

But that doesn't mean it was all easy by that point. Logan had several therapies a week, sometimes two or three in one day. I was juggling work and being a mom while managing all his needs. Do you know how hard it is to see your child strapped into an apparatus that looks like an ancient Chinese torture device, just to get him to simulate what it feels like to be upright?! Oh my God, it was awful...the bloodcurdling screams this kid would let out broke my heart and brought tears to my eyes at times. But it was necessary, fighting and pushing through was necessary for his success and for him to overcome so many deficiencies. He would just have to work longer and harder for things. And Kevin and I were up for the challenge because we always knew that his day would come, and we knew Logan would overcome anything else that came at him. He didn't beat cancer before he was a year old to not overcome everything else he would have to face. While my husband and I—along with Logan's medical team—firmly believed that Logan would catch up, it was still very hard to accept that he wouldn't reach the "normal" childhood milestones at the same times as other kids, if at all. Eating on his own, saying "Mommy" or "Daddy," asking for a snack, playing cars or blocks, playing house and making breakfast in a play kitchen, or even helping me in the real kitchen—these things hadn't happened, and we knew they may never happen. But we always tried to stay as positive as we could, and we stayed focused on the good. Logan was walking, his communication was getting better, he was tolerating his feeds, and he was doing well in his therapies. We just had to stay optimistic and capitalize on his successes. Just like we had made it through his treatment by staying positive, we would continue that same way. There was no other option! He would have a lot to prove to this world, to the medical world and his medical team, and honestly, to my husband and me. There would be times when I thought he didn't understand, and sure enough, he would do what I had asked. I might just have to enunciate or explain it in a little more detail or break things down more, but he understood. He is A–M–A–Z–I–N–G! (Did I say that yet?!)

I am a firm believer that everything happens for a reason, but sometimes, I just wanted to be able to go to work, come home, make dinner, and have my family eat together. Or just pick up and go to the park without having to worry about Logan's feeding time or if he might hit another kid at the park because he can't communicate well. I've always known we were meant to help him overcome all of the obstacles that have constantly been thrown at him, but boy...it was exhausting! Yes, he's a good kid, and he was gradually becoming more independent, but it was still really fucking hard. I never got all of my stuff done, whether it was work, tasks for the Logan Strong™ Foundation, or household chores. I swear, the second he saw me sit down on the couch with my laptop or start folding laundry, he would attack me, hitting, biting, or scratching me. It was very frustrating, and I'm not naturally a patient person, so the only patience I had was always reserved for him. There had been several times when people had offered to help or take something off my plate, but unfortunately, any time I agreed, I was disappointed with how it was done and I just ended up doing it myself anyway. So, needless to say, my time was very limited!

And in the early part of 2020, we encountered a totally new hiccup—okay, it wasn't a hiccup, it was a *huge* issue we had with Logan's school and how he was being fed. I'm sharing this here not to get anyone in trouble but to share just one of the many things we had to deal with, and to give a glimpse into some of the challenges we had to face. When Logan had started school in September 2019, we had to have the doctor rewrite his prescription numerous times to fit the school nurse's needs. At the time, Logan had been getting fed five times a day (every three hours). We eventually got the script written and everything was going well. But by mid-October, it was brought to our attention that Logan had been missing one hour of school per day, which equated to a full day of school missed per week, because he was getting fed twice a day at school (at approximately thirty minutes each feed). This was eye-opening to us, and we knew it was very important to come up with a resolution. After working with Logan's nutritionists and doctors to come up with a solution, we were able to switch

Logan to four feeds a day (every four hours). The new regimen was going well, even when a new school nurse started. We were mixing Logan's formula at home and sending it in a bottle for his school feed, and the doctor's script had been written specifically to accommodate for this feed.

Then in January 2020, another new school nurse started. She fed Logan on Monday and Tuesday, and I was then called into the office on Wednesday. The new nurse said she was uncomfortable feeding Logan from the bottles I was sending, and she said that by law she would need to see the label. I responded by saying that that wouldn't be possible because of the way the mix was done. We continued to go back and forth trying to figure out how everyone would be happy, and we both agreed we would do some digging to find a reasonable solution. The nurse then called in sick on Thursday and quit on Friday (via text), leaving us to deal with this "law" she had brought to everyone's attention. To make matters worse, Logan's new LPN had no problem feeding him the pre-mix that we had been sending in a bottle, but because this issue had been brought to the attention of the school and the district, they could no longer allow it.

Based on this "law," (and I use "law" in quotation marks because it's not clearly defined anywhere), the school nurse would have to administer tube-fed formula from a container with a label. We wouldn't have had a problem with this if Logan were being fed from a single package per feed. But the problem was that we were making Logan's formula the night before for the next day's four feeds. It consisted of three 300-milliliter packages of Compleat, one 1.5-ounce package of Benecalorie, and 200 milliliters of water. This would then be split into four 270- milliliter feeds for the next day. If his formula had come in individual servings with labels, I would have had no problem having the nurse feed him from a labeled package, but that was not possible with how his feedings were measured out.

The school tried suggesting that the nurse could make his four feeds for the day and then send the rest home. *Well, why is the nurse more competent to make Logan's feeds than me or Kevin, his parents?* Not to mention that I couldn't guarantee I could always transport his feeds back home because he sometimes had therapy, doctors' appointments, or day care, which meant we would get home late, and his formula needed to be refrigerated within four hours and only had a twenty-four-hour shelf life.

To appease the school and to abide by this "law," we decided to just send in a packet of Compleat for the school nurse to feed him each day. It was a 300- milliliter package, and he only got 210 milliliters with 60 milliliters of water for his school feed, which meant not only were we wasting 90 milliliters of his formula, but it also made his other three feeds for the day thicker. More than half the time, he was getting sick after his morning feed because his body was not used to the thicker consistency, and this was *completely* (no pun intended) defeating the purpose of him going to feeding therapy, which he had started about a month earlier.

Not knowing what to do or how to fix this major issue, I spoke with several people at the school, the school district, tube feeding organizations, and other "tubie" moms. We even tried speaking with the New York State Education Department, who in turn, told us that we needed to speak with the New York State Board of Nursing. I also called our assemblywoman and a lawyer for advice. Logan's team of doctors, his nutritionist, and his case manager were all behind us on this and were also researching a possible solution.

This went on for almost three weeks, and I was so frustrated and upset. I just wanted my child to be fed the way he needed his nutrition. Why was this any different than a child bringing in a bagged lunch? I was not (and am still not) arguing the fact that, per law, a licensed nurse had to feed him in school. The problem was that the procedure by which he was being fed was considered medical (in a school setting), and all medicine required a label. But this wasn't *medicine*—the contents of the formula were *nutrition*. If it had been medicine, I would understand why they would need a labeled bottle and a script from the doctor. In my eyes, this was discrimination. My son was being discriminated against because he couldn't eat by mouth yet, and the "law" was dictating what and how he was fed. How should this have trumped Logan's nutritional needs?! We researched and read about many laws and regulations on the state level, and some were contradictory while others only stated "best practices." To me, "best practices" are guidelines, not hard-and-fast rules. We couldn't be the only family in the state of New York whose child was being tube-fed from a pre-mixed formula at school. (And, as it turned out, we were not, and I had proof from other school districts.) But because that one nurse who had worked with Logan for all of *three days* had caused a stink, we now had to fight this "law" that contradicted itself!

It seemed like such a simple fix—feed the child based on his doctor's orders—and yet it was anything but simple to resolve. My husband and I missed countless hours—if not *days*—of work between making phone calls, sending emails, reading and researching regulations and laws, and sometimes even going to Logan's school to feed him ourselves. How was this in anyone's best interest?! Eventually, we had to put a pause on our fight when COVID hit in March 2020 and all schools were shut down. I had enough respect for what was happening around the world that I stopped fighting and making calls regarding his feeding issue. Once the school reopened, I just sent in his packet of formula and abided by the "law." COVID precautions were more important than our feeding issue, and at least Logan was getting fed. I've learned to pick my battles through this journey!

The United States—and the rest of the world—had been struck with a pandemic, and everything literally shut down. There was no school, no work (for me, at least; my husband was deemed an essential worker because he works for a non-profit that serves the homeless and poor populations in our area), no extracurricular activities, no therapies, and doctors' appointments only if they were necessary (but those were even canceled or done via Zoom). I was so thankful that I had decided to step down from management in January 2020. It was like the universe had once again had my back. If I had had a team of agents underneath me at that time, I don't know what I would have done. There was no way in hell I could have managed and kept a team of commission-only sales reps motivated. Thank you, universe!

The world shut down and I became a stay-at-home mother, teacher, and therapist overnight. To transition into my new roles, I created a school corner in our dining room, organized a binder with tabs for each class (or therapy), and created a daily schedule. Well, that lasted about three days before I became so stressed and overwhelmed. I reached out to Logan's developmental pediatrician, Dr. Lucas, and she told me to throw it all out; throw away the schedule and just be a mom and do what I can. I was shocked.

I said, "But how will he learn and continue to develop and grow? What about his therapies and everything else?"

Dr. Lucas explained that Logan would learn naturally by exploring, experimenting, and creating on his own. And if I was stressed out and overwhelmed, he would sense that and would feel that way as well. Another thing she said to me that really resonated was that we had been through so much already, and I deserved to enjoy just being a mom.

I said, "You are absolutely right."

I then wrote myself a script that said, "F it all!" and I put that in the front sleeve of the binder. And that was how we survived an international pandemic!

CHAPTER
17

SOMETIME AROUND LOGAN'S fourth birthday, he had become very...how do I say it... Truth be told, he was a pain in the ass for a good month! He was biting, kicking, hitting, banging his head, and pulling my hair. He wouldn't sit for his feeds, and he screamed whenever we took him into the bathroom to go potty. *Did he have a headache? A belly-ache? Were his molars coming in?* This was all especially hard because he couldn't tell us what was wrong. We spoke with his school, wondering if there had been any significant changes there. Nope. We spoke with his gastro team, his neuro team, and his peds team, but they didn't have any concrete answers.

Finally, when we asked his developmental pediatrician, Dr. Lucas, she said this was "normal" behavior for Logan whenever he has been on the verge of a breakthrough! When I heard her say this, I cried tears of joy, especially when she said she thought that the breakthrough was going to be language. This was *huge* considering that in January of that past year Dr. Lucas had said she was unsure if Logan would ever be able to talk!

By the time Logan's fourth birthday was on the horizon, he was doing so well. His language was exploding! His communication had gotten so much better, and he was using more sign language as well. He knew how to ask for help using sign, which was absolutely adorable because the sign for "help" is one hand flat with your other hand in a fist with your thumb up and you raise both hands together, but Logan would actually do this using prayer hands and say, "Help"! It was cute and powerful! We still had a long road ahead of us, but this kid has always been such a fighter!

We still tried so hard to bring normalcy to Logan's world, and his birthday celebration was just another example of how hard this could be at times. On the night before his birthday, I was blowing up a large balloon in the shape of the number four when it suddenly popped, and a breakdown ensued, not because the balloon had popped but because of what it meant to me to have that large number four balloon in his room when he woke up on his birthday. To me, it meant a sense of normalcy, celebration, and love. My husband, being the supporter he is, said we would get another balloon the next day, and he continued to blow up smaller balloons in the hope of making me feel better. The next day, Logan's Aunt Tommie came to the rescue with a large number four balloon! Once again, I thanked God for our support system of amazing people who love Logan and have helped us get through every challenge, big and small.

We had to cancel Logan's actual birthday party because of COVID and were instead going to just have a small family gathering, but the infection rates were so scary at the time so we opted for a Mommy and Daddy day with Logan. We enjoyed a family day together at home, relaxing, playing downstairs in his ball pit, and watching Logan play on his iPad. We also celebrated with Logan's best friends, Noah and Pierson, and their mom and dad, Bridget and Mark. We always have so much fun together, and those boys are so good with Logan!

For Thanksgiving and Christmas 2020, we again kept everything small while also trying for as much normalcy as possible. But it sucked because Christmas morning wasn't really exhilarating like it usually is for little kids. Logan didn't know any different. He didn't understand the excitement of waking up on Christmas morning to presents that had been left by a fat man in a suit! We tried to engage him in opening presents, but he just didn't get it. In moments like those, all I can do is be grateful that our son is with us and pray for the day when he can enjoy those holidays—and I know he will!

By January 2021, I was still working from home because the world hadn't opened back up just yet, and Logan was in school part-time. I knew I wanted to write a book—this book—because I needed to share our journey: the highs and lows, the struggles and successes, but most of all, the journey of our miracle boy! I started by researching how to write a book, then I spoke with several people, including a few published writers, to see what I'd need to do. Finally, I learned that the first step is to just *write*! Well, that was easier said than done. It's not that I didn't have plenty to say; I just didn't have (or couldn't seem to find) the time to do so. Juggling a special-needs toddler during a pandemic while trying to work was insane! I was so thankful that I had stepped down from management a year earlier to focus on Logan and his needs. I don't know what I would have done if I had had a team of agents reporting to me while I was homeschooling that crazy kid! The universe had my back on that one. Even so, it was such a struggle for me to find time to write because I still always had a million balls in the air and I felt like I was constantly running. I struggled a lot to find balance and time for everything. But I was so excited to start on this book, so I decided to go away with a business associate and friend for a little retreat getaway at a beautiful hotel with a lake view. It wasn't easy for me to be apart from Logan, but my goal was to get my book outline done, and I did just that!

On Logan's fourth cancerversary, I tried to stay busy just as I always did in the years before. This day never got any easier, but this time was special because I had received a message from God (on a Facebook page that posts spiritual messages) and it couldn't be more fitting for the day: *Today, Jennifer, God wants you to know that it is time to finally forgive yourself. You've carried the guilt and the shame for long enough. You've kept your wounds open for long enough. The time has come to let go, to heal. Keep the lessons and let the pain heal. Yes, you know what we are talking about.*

So, on Logan's fourth cancerversary, I looked back on everything we had gone through—all the fear, turmoil, and pain—but this time I felt like I was finally ready to hear that message I had received from God. I felt like I was finally ready to begin letting go and allowing those old wounds to heal. A new sense of acceptance started to take shape in my heart. I used to wonder, if I had been twenty years old when this happened, would I have been able to handle it like I did? I now knew in my gut the answer was *no*! It had all unfolded just as it had been meant to happen. If I had been younger, I wouldn't have had the experience or connections I had to get us through this. I am truly grateful that Logan chose me to be his mom, and that he chose us to be his parents. We are the blessed ones to experience the miracle of this child and his determination and development! Don't get me wrong, this journey is *hard*—I mean, *really fucking hard*! But it has also taught me patience, love, hope, faith, and resilience— just to name a few. We would not have gotten so far without those values. We had been told from day one that our son wouldn't survive (several times). Then they said he would never walk, and they said that he would probably never talk. But that was *never* an option for us. We didn't know any different but to fight and to keep moving forward with every ounce of love we could give to our son. Logan felt all of this, and he knew that he had to fight too—and he did, and he *won*! Talking, eating, and potty training were our focuses now, and we knew he would succeed, just like he's done with every worst-case scenario that's ever been thrown at him. I can't tell you how *amazing* it felt to finally know—and to trust in that knowledge—that my kid would be OK; that he would face any challenge head-on and would overcome them all. He is truly a *miracle*. I am so proud of him. He is smart, he never gives up, and he is absolutely adorable! I am super blessed to be with this kid on a daily basis.

On his fourth cancerversary, I also received a message from one of our delivery nurses, which really drove home everything I was feeling. She said, "There is not one video of Logan that does not remind me of the day he was born, and your unbelievable dedication to the thought process that no matter what he will be OK! He blew a gasket to meet you early! Thank you for believing in him and adding to my amazing stories of miracles I have witnessed at Albany Medical Center! Keep up the good work, my friend!"

Oh, and of course, Logan got his first shiner on his fourth cancerversary! He had horse therapy two days prior, and whenever he had horse therapy on Saturdays, my husband would come with us, which would allow me time to ride also. This was great therapy for me as well because it's the only time since Logan's diagnosis when I don't think about anything except for what I am doing in that moment, and that is being one with the horse. Logan would ride first and Kevin and I would walk alongside on each side of him, or I would take videos and pictures while Logan was riding. Then when Logan was done, Kevin would take him outside to run and play ball while I got my lesson (aka therapy). Well, on this particular day, Logan was running and playing with Daddy, and because Logan runs so fast, his feet tend to come out from underneath him at times. Sure enough, he fell, landed on his face, and got road rash and a shiner! This wasn't his first time having a face-plant, and I'm sure it will not be his last. Boys will be boys!

Throughout the first half of 2021 I was working part-time (mostly virtually), and I would pick up Logan from school every day before handling his therapies, taking him to his doctors' appointments, and filling out tons of paperwork for all the services he was receiving at the time. (All of that was a part-time job in itself!) He graduated preschool in June and finished summer school (an extension of his pre-K program) in the second week of August, and then I was home with him until he started kindergarten in September. Meanwhile, I was working, writing this book, and planning the fourth annual

Logan Cup (our annual golf tournament and the biggest fundraiser for the Logan Strong™ Foundation).

That summer, we took Logan to see his daddy race motorcycles for the first time in New Hampshire. He absolutely loved it. He's always loved to watch NASCAR and motorcycle races on TV, and now we were watching his daddy from the starting line! I couldn't stand to watch as Kevin went over one hundred miles an hour on turns where his knee was basically touching the ground. Logan, on the other hand, was giggling and smiling, and just had a look of pure joy as he watched the motorcycles going by. And to top it off, Kevin won his race!

We also took a trip to Maine for a couple of days with my in-laws and my mother and stepfather. I had been dying to get Logan to the ocean, and when we got there, the weather was horrible but that didn't stop us. We went to the beach in the pouring rain, and Logan absolutely loved it! We even got a beautiful family photo of us in our raincoats, holding hands, facing the ocean in the rain. It was *perfect*! I didn't even care about the weather; the experience was all that mattered. The weather wasn't so great the next day either, so we just walked around downtown and got ice cream, and of course, taffy. My mom and stepdad took us out to dinner that night for my birthday (which had been the day before) and Kevin's birthday (which had passed a week before) while my in-laws watched Logan. It was nice to get out! On the last day of our trip, the weather broke and it was gorgeous out! We took Logan right down to the beach and he just ran and ran and ran! It was the most amazing thing to see and experience. He even tried pushing the water back into the ocean; it was so cute! After going to the beach, we went back downtown and took him to the zoo, but he couldn't have cared less. That didn't even matter, though. It was all about the experience and helping him learn and grow in different situations.

After our amazing trip, as September and the new school year approached, there came one more fucking thing to present yet another new challenge. Throughout the previous few months, we had been preparing for kindergarten, which included several virtual meetings, conversations with teachers and therapists, and chatting with the doctors to get the appropriate scripts and evaluations. One of those evaluations I hadn't been expecting, and I didn't like what we found out.

Back in June, I had received a phone call from Dr. Lucas, Logan's developmental pediatrician, after we had reached out to her regarding several behaviors (including biting, hitting, aggression, and impulsivity) that Logan had been having. She had asked his school (including his one-on-one aide), his day care, and Kevin and me to fill out a questionnaire that would help her determine the next steps. After reviewing the information and speaking with us, Dr. Lucas concluded that she wanted to test Logan for autism. I started crying as soon as I heard this. Dr. Lucas had mentioned to us a couple of years ago that she had been concerned that he may have autism, but she had quickly taken back her statement because Logan had started making appropriate eye contact and was very social. So when she made this statement to me again, I was devastated.

Thankfully, I knew I could trust Dr. Lucas completely, and I could always have an open and honest conversation with her. She was super sweet and understanding throughout the conversation, and she was even kind enough to call me and Kevin individually the next day to talk each of us through her thought process. While I didn't like that she had brought up autism again, I trusted her. And at the end of the day, I knew an autism diagnosis would only help Logan get additional services and would further support all of us as we figured out how to deal with his behaviors.

I then asked her, "How do they know it's not the brain injury?" She said, "We don't!"

When I asked her how many children with brain injuries had been diagnosed with autism, she said, simply, "A lot!"

It wasn't so much the potential autism diagnosis that bothered me; it was the fact that this was *one more fucking thing* that we had to go through, one more fucking box we would have to check for our son. Hadn't we been through enough?!

We scheduled his evaluation for the following week, and he slept through it! But it worked out anyway because it allowed Kevin and me to spend that time chatting with Dr. Lucas to understand where she was coming from, what she was thinking, and what the process would look like. Logan finally had his evaluation three weeks later, and my mommy intuition just knew we were going to get the diagnosis.

A week later, we received the paperwork in the mail, and it was confirmed: Logan now had an autism spectrum disorder (ASD) diagnosis. I didn't like it, and I truly knew in my heart and in my gut that it was the brain injury, but if it would help him get additional services, then so be it. Plus, Dr. Lucas made a good point when she said that it was better for him to have the autism diagnosis and get the help he needs with his behaviors rather than have him be labeled as defiant and not receive the necessary support. It made sense, but I still hated it. Childhood cancer had done this to my child. If he had never had a brain tumor, he would have never had to have a tumor resection where they had removed his left frontal lobe, not to mention the insane amount of chemo he had gone through. If it hadn't been for all of that, we wouldn't have even been having this conversation! *It was just one more fucking thing!* And just like we've done through everything else we had already faced, we would see Logan through this next hurdle and every other challenge to come.

CONCLUSION

WHILE THIS BOOK is coming to an end, Logan's journey—and my family's journey—is not. We will still have our highs and lows, our setbacks and comebacks, but we will always remain positive and we will always focus on the good. This journey has taught me a lot, including...

...patience. For one, my kid didn't start walking until he was almost two years old, and we are *still* working on talking and eating. We always say, "It's on Logan's time and on his terms. It will happen when he's ready!"

...resilience and perseverance, as even with the lows and setbacks, we have always adjusted and kept going.

...pure joy and happiness. When Logan does something a "normal" kid does, our happiness and excitement are amplified a thousand times. For example, the first time he said "Mommy," or "Daddy," or "I love you," or the first time he came up to me and asked for help without attacking me, these were things that "normal" kids do all the time, but the fact that my son—who is a cancer survivor with a traumatic brain injury (and now autism)—does and *can* do any of this just melts my heart. There was also the time when Logan walked down the basement stairs by himself. I was working in my office when all of a sudden I heard Logan laughing below me. I ran down the stairs *so fast* to see what was going on! I must have left the basement door open, and I had no idea he knew how to walk down the stairs by himself! And the first time I took Logan to the splash pad this summer, the place was so busy, with kids running around everywhere, and Logan loved it! He just ran and ran and ran and did not hit *anyone*, not one person. This was—and still is—a BFD (big fucking deal)!

...that love is hard. Yep, I said it. I love my son, I love my husband, and I love my family, but it's fucking hard. There are times when I think about running away. I would *never*, but I do sometimes wonder what it would be like. I don't have time for those thoughts to control me or even last long, but I am constantly reminding myself that this is *my journey*, and I was chosen for this job for a reason. To be perfectly honest, most people couldn't handle half the shit I do on a daily basis, and conversely, I don't know if I could ever handle a "normal" child—for real. How the hell do y'all do that shit?!

I am constantly learning and growing, as a mom, a wife, a daughter, a friend, a businesswoman, a nonprofit business owner, and a humanitarian. That's what life is about—learning and growing—and Logan reminds me of this every single day. If you are not learning or growing, then what is there to life?

We have never been those parents who run over to console our son whenever he falls. My thinking is, *You've beaten cancer, kid! Get the fuck up and keep running!* When he comes over and asks for help or grabs my hand to lead me somewhere to get something for him, I stop, pull my hand away, and make him do it himself. How else is he going to learn? If you fall down, you get back up. If you need something, you can do it yourself. Period. Just now, I went into the kitchen for a drink, and Logan ran up to me, grabbed my hand, and said, "Ball." I immediately responded with, "Go get it." He then looked at me and said, "Go get it," in his cute little voice. And then he went and got his ball, all on his own.

As much as we strive for normalcy, Logan has a brain injury, and it's difficult in certain situations. For example, we recently took him to a place called Christmas Land, and of course, there was a line to see Santa. We walked by and were asked if we wanted to add our name to the list. I said no because I knew Logan wouldn't stand in line. Moments like this *really* suck. We couldn't get Logan's picture taken with Santa this year because we had been quarantined for ten days (thank you, COVID), and when we finally did have the opportunity, he just didn't have the patience to wait in line. (He totally gets that from me, brain injury or not!) We often have to ask for special treatment for things like this, which part of me hates and feels bad about doing, but another part of me thinks, *Fuck it! They deserve it. Logan's been through enough, and they've been through enough, so give them whatever they want!* (Yeah, I just said that in the third person; it's more affective!)

I know that some of the people who can understand this the most are my fellow cancer moms, like Leanne, who joined me on a trip to Washington, DC, in April 2018 to advocate for the STAR Act, which helped raise federal funding for childhood cancer research. Leanne and I had met in the nourishment room at Albany Medical Center in the spring of 2017. In September that year, she lost her daughter, Avery Rose—Ava, or "her Rosebud," as Leanne called her. Leanne is a better writer than I am, and she has an amazing story to tell herself. I admire her strength and honesty! And I can't forget about Niki, another fellow cancer mom, who taught me that being marginal is OK; that it's OK to not be in management, to not go above and beyond sometimes, and that it's OK to just *be* and just *do*. Niki's daughter, Giada, was diagnosed shortly after Logan and is about six months older than he is. We had mutual friends who had wanted us to meet, but we allowed it to happen naturally (and if it wasn't for me, she would have never known of the yummy goodness of turkey day at the hospital). And, of course, there's Lorie. I mentioned her daughter, Gracie, earlier in the book. Lorie is one of the sweetest and kindest women I have ever known. We met one day during a Flashes of Hope session when the organization had come to the hospital and took family photos for the cancer families. Both Giada and Gracie are now cancer-free and treatment-free but continue to have their own struggles and issues with the aftereffects of chemotherapy. These kids are all superheroes, and these cancer moms are heroes in their own right too!

As I was finishing the final edits on this book, I realized that I had left out all the TV news interviews, articles, and media coverage we have received throughout our journey. Then I quickly realized that that's not what this book is about. But I do have to make mention of them because we are grateful for the help we've received in spreading the word about Logan's journey (and for receiving tons of love and prayers in doing so) and the importance of childhood cancer awareness. And I will continue to go on the local news every September to encourage our community to "Be Bold and Go Gold" for childhood cancer!

I'm constantly reassuring myself that this journey is ours for a reason. And I wanted to share our journey through this book because I want everyone to know that life *does* fucking suck sometimes, but it can also be filled with love and hope, and you just have to keep on going no matter what. We aren't always handed sunshine and rainbows; sometimes we're given hurricanes and tornadoes. But what comes after those disasters can be more beautiful than anything you could have ever wanted or imagined.

Trust me, I still feel lonely, hurt, angry, and upset at times. That's life. But I have the most beautiful, strongest boy on earth, and he has my heart and soul. I know that when I go to put him to bed tonight, he's probably going to pull my hair or try to rip my glasses off my face. (And he's a ninja, boy, but I'm learning to be quicker!) This is my life; this is just how it is. I can cry myself to sleep every night, or I can get up early every day and try to be a better person than I was the day before. Don't get me wrong, I have my moments, but I don't stay there long. I choose not to because I have a superhero to raise, a miracle boy to share with the world.

When I got that message from God on Logan's fourth can-cerversary, to me it meant that it was time for me to "let go and let God," literally. Stop fighting what you thought your life should have been and embrace what it *is*. Find the good in life, and in others. Have empathy and genuine compassion for others. I don't have the time or energy for mindless bick-ering or ranting. I'm using my voice for good by writing this book, sharing our story, and raising awareness about child-hood cancer.

I keep envisioning a day sometime in the future when I am speaking to a crowd of people—maybe I'm even on a book tour!—and I'm telling everyone about Logan's journey, about how we learned to have faith and trust in the power of prayer, and how life showed us that miracles *do* happen. And as I'm talking, Logan suddenly runs onto the stage and just starts chatting away! Even now, as I type these words, I can *feel* the pride and love in that moment. It's going to happen! I just know it.

For now, I embrace the wins every day, no matter how small they may be. I am proud to be Logan's mother. I was meant to be his mother, and he was meant to be my son. I love him with all that I am and all that I am not. I have my moments and my bad days, so does my husband, and honestly, so does Logan. But we have each other. We are on this journey *together*. We are in it for the long haul, and I look forward to the day when I will write the follow-up book that shares all of the new amazing things that Logan is going to do.

But tonight, I'm going to sit Logan on the potty one last time for the night, put his pajamas on, rub calming essential oils onto his feet and wrists, pray with him (it's *so cute* when he says, "Amen"), kiss him goodnight, and turn on his air purifier. And as I'm about to shut off the light and close the door, I'll say, "I love you," and Logan will say, "I wub you." Then I'll say, "Good night," and he'll say, in his perfectly adorable voice, "Mmmnight!"

HOW TO HELP

HOW CAN YOU help in the fight against childhood cancer? There are so many ways that you can support the fight! The National Cancer Institute's annual research budget of $5 billion only sets aside 4 percent for childhood cancer research. Meanwhile, new treatments for childhood cancer haven't been produced for decades. One in every eight children with cancer will not survive. *That's completely unacceptable.*

In addition to supporting research, families facing childhood cancer need more direct support. For many families, at least one parent leaves their job to take care of their child. As well as making up for lost income, families need guidance, information, and emotional support.

The Logan Strong™ Foundation (LSF) provides the following services for our families:

- Bracelet fundraiser campaigns
- Gift card program
- Ocho program
- "No Touching" signs
- T-shirt fundraising campaigns
- Amazon wish lists
- Cleaning services

LSF has several fundraisers throughout the year, including:

The Logan Cup: An annual golf tournament with opportunities for everyone, from volunteering to sponsorship and golfers. This is our biggest fundraiser of the year.

Walk 4 the Kids that Can't: One of the effects of childhood cancer for many of our kiddos is the inability to walk. Whether it's from being too sick from chemo, having a brain tumor that causes issues with walking, loss of balance, being quarantined due to high-risk health complications, muscle loss, being too weak to walk, or just being embarrassed and not wanting to go outside, the list can go on. With this fundraiser, The Logan Strong Foundation encourages everyone to walk for the kids who can't, while helping raise funds for our foundation. A mile a day goes a long way!

Giving Tuesday: The Tuesday after Thanksgiving has become a day to promote nonprofit organizations. Held primarily through social media, this event encourages individuals to donate to the foundation with potential matches through employers and other groups.

$10 4 $10K: During the first ten days of October, this is a social media activity that encourages donors to simply donate ten dollars while encouraging their friends to do the same.

Looking to do more? Below are examples of how you can help in different ways. Donations always help, but that's not the only way you can help in the fight!

Learn about childhood cancer. The more you learn about types of childhood cancer, the number of children it affects, and the current treatments, the better an advocate you will be.

Show your Gold. Gold is the color of the ribbon to symbolize childhood cancer. While September is Childhood Cancer Awareness month, you can also show your gold throughout the year. When you get asked about the gold ribbon, help raise awareness by talking about statistics, facts, and stories.

Volunteer. Foundations dedicated to the fight against childhood cancer are often understaffed and overwhelmed, especially small, local foundations. Donations are important, but pitching in can be even more important. Find out how you can help; it can be as simple as writing a newsletter or helping plan a fundraiser. If you personally know of an affected family, reach out and offer to help. Join advocacy fundraisers, such as St. Baldrick's Day where volunteers raise money by volunteering to shave their heads. You'd be surprised by how far just a few hours of your time can really go!

Attend fundraising events. There are so many fundraising opportunities available at any time of year. Go golfing, do a polar bear swim, shave your head, eat out at sponsoring restaurants, or participate in a silent auction. These fundraising events do more than just raise money for the foundations; they also help raise awareness through their marketing of the events. Having a great time while raising money and awareness? Of course!

Donate. Donating money is always welcome. With local, small foundations, there's less overhead, which means that more of your donation goes directly to the cause. You can often see the direct impact that your donation has on your local community.

Learn more at https://LoganStrongFoundation.org/.

RESOURCES

BELOW IS A list of the resources available for families dealing with cancer, both within the Capital Region of New York and nationally. A complete list, including camps, sibling resources, and resources for specific types of cancer, is available at the website for the Melodies Center for Childhood Cancer and Blood Disorders (https://community.amc.edu/melodies).

Aflac Cancer and Blood Disorders Center of Children's Healthcare of Atlanta: The Center is a national leader in pediatric cancer and blood disorders treatment and research. As one of the largest pediatric hematology/

oncology programs, the Center is home to one of the largest clinical trial programs in the nation. Ranked a Top 10 program by U.S. News and World Report, the Aflac Cancer and Blood Disorders Center cares for children and young adults with a wide range of cancer and blood disorders—from the most common to those rarely seen outside of the top centers. To learn more or get involved, please visit https://www.choa.org/jointhefight.

American Cancer Society (ACS): For nearly one hundred years, the (ACS) has worked relentlessly to save lives and create a world with less cancer and more birthdays. In addition to helping people stay well and get well, finding cures, and fighting back against cancer, the Capital Region ACS also supports the HopeClub.

American Childhood Cancer Organization (ACCO): The ACCO is a certified nonprofit organization focused on research and support for those affected by childhood cancers.

Cancer Care: Cancer Care provides free professional support services to individuals, families, caregivers, and the bereaved to help them cope with and manage the emotional and practical challenges of cancer.

Candlelighters: Candlelighters provides emotional, educational, and practical support to children with cancer and their families. In addition, Candlelighters helps promote childhood cancer awareness and the need for childhood cancer education and research.

Children's Oncology Group (COG): The COG, a National Cancer Institute-supported clinical trials group, is the world's largest organization devoted exclusively to childhood and adolescent cancer research.

National Cancer Institute: The National Cancer Institute supports a variety of programs focused on the cause, diagnosis, prevention, and treatment of cancer, rehabilitation from cancer, and the continuing care of cancer patients and the families of cancer patients.

St. Baldrick's Foundation: The St. Baldrick's Foundation supports research efforts to find cures for childhood cancers and give survivors long and healthy lives. Their main fundraiser is St. Baldrick's Day, where individuals collect donations by volunteering to shave their heads.

Local Organizations in the New York Capital Region

Amazing Gracie's Gift Foundation: Aims to provide gifts of support to families of children with cancer or a terminal illness. They will provide gifts of monetary donations to families in need of financial assistance and/or gifts to create memories for needy families of children with cancer or a terminal illness.

Brave Will Foundation: The mission of the Brave Will Foundation is to provide services and support for children with life-threatening illnesses and their families until a cure can be found. The foundation strives to take a family-centered approach to all aspects of palliative care and ensure that the needs of the child and his/her family are being met throughout all stages of care.

Capital Region Childhood Cancer Coalition (CRCCC): As a collaborative team, the CRCCC strives to educate, inform, and provide solutions on local childhood cancer issues while also supporting children afflicted with cancer, and their families, at the Bernard and Millie Duker Children's Hospital at Albany Medical Center.

Catie Hoch Foundation: The Catie Hoch Foundation was established in memory of Catie Hoch, a Clifton Park girl who died from neuroblastoma, an aggressive form of pediatric cancer. This foundation is dedicated to helping kids take a break from cancer. Until Catie's death in May 2000, she was very involved in establishing the purposes of the foundation, making sure that her favorite places were included on the list of things that kids in treatment should do.

Logan Strong™ Foundation: Our mission is to raise childhood cancer awareness and provide items of comfort and support for children and families while they are fighting cancer in and out of the hospital.

Maddie's Mark: Maddie's Mark is a not-for-profit foundation dedicated to helping people enjoy their "best days ever."

Myles of Smiles Foundation: The Myles of Smiles Foundation helps put happy faces in needed places for families in the northeastern United States facing life-threatening challenges.

Ronald McDonald House Charities of the Capital Region: The Ronald McDonald House provides a "home away from home" for families of seriously ill children receiving treatment at Albany Medical Center and other hospitals as well as provides the Ronald McDonald House family room at the children's hospital at Albany Med.

Rosie's Love: Rosie's Love is a 501(c)(3) not-for-profit organization committed to helping the children and families at the Melodies Center for Childhood Cancer and Blood Disorders at the Bernard and Millie Duker Children's Hospital at Albany Medical Center.

Starlight Children's Foundation: The mission of the Starlight Children's Foundation is to brighten the lives of seriously ill children. Each year, Starlight serves over 200,000 critically, chronically, and terminally ill children throughout New York, New Jersey, and Connecticut. In addition to granting wishes for sick children, Starlight provides programs on hospital pediatric wards, funds special projects for hospitalized children, and conducts a variety of outpatient activities. Starlight's goal is to help seriously ill children experience the simple joys of being a child.

Tyler DeMarco Foundation: The Tyler DeMarco Foundation's mission is inspired by Tyler's love, compassion, and determination to change the course of childhood cancer for other children who will follow. Throughout his tragic personal experiences, Tyler declared that "no kid should have to go through this."

ABOUT THE AUTHOR

JENNIFER F. HENDRICKS-FOGG is an independent benefits consultant with Aflac, and the founder and president of the Logan Strong Foundation which provides support services to pediatric cancer patients and their families. She is also a Rotarian, and she serves on the board of eba Center for Dance and Movement. Jennifer lives in Scotia, New York, with her husband, Kevin, and their son, Logan, who is their very own "tiny miracle."

To read Jen's latest blog posts about Logan's journey, visit https://LoganStrong.org/.

To learn more about the Logan Strong Foundation, visit https://LoganStrongFoundation.org/.

To view a photo album documenting Logan's journey, visit https://LoganStrong.org/tiny-miracles/ or scan the following QR code.

Made in United States
North Haven, CT
02 August 2022